Rethinking Workplace Learning and Development

RETHINKING BUSINESS AND MANAGEMENT

The Rethinking Business and Management series is a forum for innovative scholarly writing from across all substantive fields within business and management. The series aims to enrich scholarly inquiry by promoting a cutting-edge approach to management theory and analysis.

Despite the old maxim that nothing is new under the sun, it is nevertheless true that organisations evolve and contexts in which businesses operate change. Business and Management faces new and previously unforeseen challenges, responds to shifting motivations, and is shaped by competing interests and experiences. Academic scrutiny and challenge is an essential component in the development of business theory and practice and the act of rethinking and re-examining principles and precepts that may have been long held is imperative.

Rethinking Business and Management showcases authored books that address their field from a new angle, expose the weaknesses of existing frameworks, or 're-frame' the topic in some way. This might be through the integration of perspectives from other fields or even other disciplines, through challenging existing paradigms, or simply through a level of analysis that elevates or sharpens our understanding of a subject. While each book takes its own approach, all the titles in the series use an analytical lens to open up new thinking.

Titles in this series include:

Rethinking Global Value Chains and Corporate Social Responsibility
Peter Lund-Thomsen

Rethinking Workplace Learning and Development
Karen E. Watkins and Victoria J. Marsick

Rethinking Workplace Learning and Development

Karen E. Watkins

Department of Lifelong Education, Administration and Policy, University of Georgia, USA

Victoria J. Marsick

Department of Adult and Organizational Leadership, Teachers College, Columbia University, USA

RETHINKING BUSINESS AND MANAGEMENT

Edward Elgar PUBLISHING

Cheltenham, UK • Northampton, MA, USA

Published by
Edward Elgar Publishing Limited
The Lypiatts
15 Lansdown Road
Cheltenham
Glos GL50 2JA
UK

Edward Elgar Publishing, Inc.
William Pratt House
9 Dewey Court
Northampton
Massachusetts 01060
USA

A catalogue record for this book
is available from the British Library

Library of Congress Control Number: 2023939582

This book is available electronically in the **Elgar**online
Business subject collection
http://dx.doi.org/10.4337/9781802203776

Printed on elemental chlorine free (ECF)
recycled paper containing 30% Post-Consumer Waste

ISBN 978 1 80220 376 9 (cased)
ISBN 978 1 80220 377 6 (eBook)

Printed and bound in the USA

We dedicate this book first and foremost to our families – Tyson Watkins and Nguyen Dinh and Tanya, Aaron, Ethan, Dimitri, and Lily DaMommio along with Peter Neaman, Adam Neaman, Bianca Santomasso, Owen, and Olivia.

Contents

Figures

Tables

Boxes

Acknowledgments

Victoria and I would like to give a very special thanks to the learning and development practitioners who shared their work in these pages. They inspire us and help us expand our vision of learning in the workplace. We would also like to acknowledge our colleagues—especially (in alphabetical order) Laura Bierema, Pierre Faller, Seung Hyun Han, Terrence Maltbia, Aliki Nicolaides, Amra Sabic-El-Rayess, and Lyle Yorks—for all they have done to encourage our thinking. Our students have also advanced our thinking—working beside us to develop and extend these ideas through their own scholarship and helping us build a bridge to practice. A very special thanks to Dyan Holt and Peter Neaman for their unflagging and very helpful editorial support.

1. Introducing learning in complexity

This book is about rethinking workplace learning and development (L&D), and what is driving these shifts, especially the complexity and uncertainty that characterize our pandemic and post-pandemic workplaces. In this chapter, we look at this complexity and why it demands rethinking L&D.

Learning in the workplace remains tightly tied to organizational needs. It also develops valuable resources of social and knowledge capital. Over the last few decades, workplace L&D has moved from a peripheral, expendable activity in organizations to a significant player in advancing the organization's agendas. No longer first cut in an economic downturn, L&D now has a seat at the table. In these pages we show how creative practitioners have taken up the newly significant value-added mission they deliver.

A FOCUS ON COMPLEXITY

This book explores questions that L&D practitioners and scholars are asking themselves and the organizations they serve or study as they grapple with rethinking L&D at work, and how to best design, support, and sustain it. There are a number of philosophical, social, economic, cultural, or organizational lenses that can be used to drive rethinking of L&D. We have chosen, in this book, to prioritize the lens of complexity dynamics because it centers the inherent non-linear, interactive, relational unpredictability of L&D when placed within the context of knowledge-based work and organizations.[1] All L&D is not designed by organizations, nor is learning always in their control. Yet it is also the case that design influences what and how people learn—the design of jobs, the design of climates and cultures, the design of work organizations, and environmental connections among organizations in the service of work. Design signals some degree of intentionality, but such intentionality does not have to signal attempts to control the unfolding of human learning at work. We are further interested in organizations as they have moved into knowledge and creative work. Our models of informal and incidental learning, and of learning organizations and cultures, have been fed by the spring of adaptive work and circumstances that moved learning out of the primary realm of standardization and routine into the realms of discovery, exploration, and experimentation.

We are guided in our thinking about complexity and its influence on design by Ann Pendleton-Jullian and John Seely Brown (2018a). They trace fundamental shifts in science that influence organizational thinking such as the reductionism—still prevalent in some work settings where routine and standardization prevail—guided by Newton's laws of physics concerning complicated systems encoded in rules and laws. They call for a different paradigm that explains contingencies dependent on organisms' histories. Darwin's evolutionary theory helped us to understand that "process is more important than law in shaping living systems" (p. 33).

Ecology centers on ecosystems, which are complex in nature. "The word *complex* comes from the Latin root *plecetere*: "to weave, entwine" (p. 35). Ecosystems grow through "autocatalytic mutualism" in which "the system is constantly generating an increase of energy and matter to sustain or grow itself from within. It does this by relying upon the mutual dependencies at work" (p. 35). This

> allows us to see beyond classical notions of competition to a living system driven more by collaboration in a contingent context; evolution and resiliency that are dependent upon chance and novel perturbations; and propensities rather than causal processes or fixed laws; mak[ing] ecology a productive third window through which to see the world anew. (p. 37)

Ecologies can be social, mental, and physical. Pendleton-Jullian and Brown draw on ecology to advocate design unbound and designing for emergence, which also calls for a new definition of agency. They note:

> When we look at problems as only scientific or technical in nature, removed from the contexts to which they are responding, they may be *complicated*, but they generally can be solved through straightforward, scientific and engineering design methods. But, when we understand these problems as embedded within human contexts that organize themselves through changing social, political, economic, and cultural belief systems, we are in the realm of *complexity*.
>
> *Complex systems* are found in the transitional space between order and chaos; they are charged by their potential to slip into chaos while human nature works desperately to tame them into order. Poised between ordered and chaotic systems, complex systems are brimming with potential at all times. (2018a, p. 45)

The idea that complex systems are charged with potential is quite evident in the stories we share from a range of L&D practitioners and scholars with whom we have talked and/or whose work we have read. As we do so, we will discuss where we see these efforts opening up space to develop capacities suited to this world of emergence in which workers live, learn, and perform. A challenge with complexity is that "any attempt to create a solution changes the nature of the problems … [that call for] provisional actions to work on the problem . . . [that, in turn] creates unintended consequences that change the nature of the problem" (Pendleton-Jullian & Brown, 2018a, p. 48). Pendleton-Jullian and Brown further conclude that, "although not solvable in any traditional sense, complex problems *can be worked on* by affecting the way the complex system—the context—around the problem evolves." We can also act in the situation by intentionally making things and taking actions that "interact with the emergent change in the system" in order to affect its "emergent relational properties." Thus, we can (1) alter the boundaries of the system, influencing the scope and constraints of the system; and (2) introduce "probes" to "audit the system as it is changing"; or (3) "create modulators" that can influence changes in the system (p. 48). The probes and modulators often interact as they give and receive information and act on new knowledge.

L&D architects in this book illustrate a range of actions in and on the system as they experiment with alternative approaches to workplace learning. We will use this lens of complexity to ask of these examples whether and how their rethinking of L&D opens new ground in complex circumstances.

The redefinition of contextual system boundaries for L&D—and its further shaping through use of probes and modulators—is illustrated by the authors of vignettes in our chapters. These L&D leaders are altering the boundaries of the systems in which they work. Our early conception of workplace learning was built on the blurring of boundaries across what had initially been conceived of as somewhat separate disciplines joined together to comprise human resource development (HRD). We instead imagined a cone in which the base consisted of the interaction of formal and informal learning, which was enacted in multiple embedded and interactive learning levels: individual, group, organizational, and professions. Our cone did not blur these boundaries as thoroughly as they are blended today under banners such as "talent management" or "connectors" or other titles suited to the integrated way in which L&D functions in evolving organizational work designs. But the vignettes in this book suggest that L&D is going into cross-functional spaces where perhaps brave individuals feared to go in industrial and post-industrial enterprises.

Some influences affecting rethinking L&D seem particularly strong—especially technology. Perhaps none has been as significant as the pivot to digital delivery during the pandemic. In the vignette below, Molly Nagler, Chief Learning Officer at PepsiCo, illustrates how the pivot changed assumptions about learner control, the quality of online learning, and the power of the digital context for embedding cultural changes. In making these changes, PepsiCo managed the complexity and uncertainty of the pandemic.

BOX 1.1 TOSSING ASSUMPTIONS OUT: SHIFTING PEPSICO'S LEARNING PROGRAMS ONLINE

Molly Nagler, Chief Learning Officer, PepsiCo

COVID-19 took everyone by surprise in 2020, especially those of us who had spent most of our careers in an office. Suddenly, we'd gone from interacting with one another in person to sitting behind our computers alone at home. Thus began our efforts to craft an entirely different approach to learning and working.

We initially paused and postponed instructor-led learning for professional employees, including our flagship programs that we didn't think could be effective online. But as the days, weeks, and months went by, the workplace as we once knew it remained dormant.

So, we asked ourselves, "What are we capable of doing online?" In hindsight, it's odd to think we ever doubted just how much we could accomplish virtually. However, we wanted to understand how we could continue to provide learning opportunities regardless of where our employees were—in an office, in a plant, or at home. And as the expectations around the current workplace continued to shift, we questioned our own assumptions.

We quickly mobilized to roll out existing and new online courses, while maintaining our peer cohort structure and evolving programming along the way.

Experiments and Lessons Learned

- *On-demand learning.* Shortly after the shutdown, we launched a global Learner Experience Platform, a one-stop shop where learners can access internal assets, search through a content library, and create their own learning pathways. The platform uses Artificial Intelligence (AI) to suggest content based on the learner's interests and goals. We've also been able to maintain a pulse on what's top of mind for our learners, helping us to create new content in response to that appetite.
- *Non-traditional topics.* We saw an unmet need to discuss topics that aren't generally covered in professional settings, including mental health and even grief. We also put more emphasis on emotional intelligence, leading through a crisis, and empathy. One initiative was the multi-part "Take Care" webinar series featuring notable experts from outside our organization, including a Buddhist teacher.
- *Creating community.* When we went virtual, we assumed chat capabilities would be a disruption to our learning (like whispering across the

table in a traditional classroom) but quickly learned it had the opposite effect. The chat was where learners built a temporary community to experience the program together and learn from each other. Learners asked questions, shared stories, and received support from their colleagues. Open communication is critical, and this was a powerful way to let learners share their personal stories and connect with others who were navigating similar experiences.

- *Real-time evaluations*. We often feel the need to collect and provide feedback following a learning opportunity. But in 2020, the last thing our learners wanted to do was another task. Instead, we checked in regularly within our chats and gathered real-time feedback.
- *Simplicity*. We made an intentional decision to avoid any fancy online platforms for instructor-led learning and instead adopted Zoom, even though it is not purpose-built for learning. Instead of toggling between multiple platforms, learners could seamlessly transition from a meeting to a learning session within the same platform. We wanted to challenge our learners with new ideas and concepts, not with tricky logins and tech functionality! As with any event (in person or otherwise), trial-and-error is common, but we were able to uncover different functions and improve the experience for everyone.
- *Scale*. Scaling is crucial to operating a global company, and it's much easier to scale when you're operating online. We can now offer career milestone programs like First-Time Manager dozens of times a year and in different time zones. In fact, we had an unprecedented 11,000 virtual training registrations in May 2022. Going online resulted in more reach and less spend.

The Future of Learning and Development

This experience taught us the need to be creative and stay true to the values we have as an organization. At PepsiCo, we are preparing the next generation of leaders to lead with purpose. Purpose is part of our mission, and it's an anchor within our learning and development programs.

Through learning, we've been able to communicate that approach to "Leading with Purpose." We believe that everyone has a purpose, and through our learning programs we invite our colleagues to reflect on their own sense of purpose and create ways to bring that to life through their roles within the organization.

Much like diversity, equity, and inclusion (DEI), purpose is part of a company's maturity curve. When companies first started talking about DEI, it was a stand-alone effort driven by one executive or department. Today, it's woven within the fabric of any major leadership program, and we believe purpose is headed in that same direction.

We also believe in championing strategic skills at all levels. The revolution of upskilling and reskilling has quickly gained speed. It's the idea of expanding your hiring pool beyond the obvious candidates and giving someone the skills they need to succeed once they've been hired, vs. expecting them to walk in with skills in hand. This is a game changer for the war on talent and practicing equitable, inclusive hiring. Learning teams are working more closely with talent acquisition teams to have conversations around the types of skills we need to then promote them internally through learning resources.

One of our reskilling and upskilling initiatives, "My Education," gives more than 100,000 frontline and professional U.S.-based associates financial support to develop their capabilities and take their careers in a new direction. Employees who've been with the company for at least six months can go back to school and access more than a hundred flexible education and upskilling programs at no cost to them.

I envision a near future where skill adjacencies result in more upskilling and reskilling for current employees. It's complex, but companies are calling on us as leadership and development professionals to rethink what we once knew and uncover some of the greatest assets already within our organizations.

It is clear that the complexity, and particularly the uncertainty about what lies ahead, is calling L&D professionals to rethink assumptions about their work. Their willingness to do so and the creativity of their responses have proven to be great assets.

OVERVIEW OF THIS BOOK

This book begins by looking at the nature of L&D in the workplace, as well as current and future trends. The book then takes a deeper dive into our work around informal and incidental learning, team learning, and the learning organization, and how these are evolving in the face of complexity. Finally, the book looks at implications of this rethinking for leadership and learning analytics as critical functions in L&D.

How does L&D—which originated in certainties, best practices, and training to acquire skills guaranteed to make one successful using top-down, organizationally controlled push models—support learners in Volatile, Uncertain, Complex, and Ambiguous (VUCA) environments through bottom-up, pull models propelled by learner passion and purpose? Designers, developers, and leaders are modifying subject matter expert-centered instructional systems design approaches for everyone-centered design thinking and digitally driven partnerships. This book describes these shifts in L&D. In this section, we preview key points in each chapter with respect to what is being rethought—underlying assumptions or conceptualizations about learning, creation of new practices or processes, or tweaks to existing ways of doing things using intelligent technologies. We ask: What is new in rethinking L&D? How does complexity affect rethinking?

The PepsiCo story in this chapter captures a recurring theme emphasized in complexity science—that is, "sensitive dependence on initial conditions" often captured by the idea of the butterfly effect because of the interdependence within a system (Glasner & Weiss, 1993). COVID-19 touched off a pandemic pivot that accelerated L&D's move to online learning. In Chapter 2 we examine fundamental conceptualizations of learning and of HRD. Chapter 3 focuses on the impact of technology: the growth of intelligent technologies that opened the door to satisfying a relentless need and desire for learning and skilling. By using technology in new ways, Bank of America (BOA) created active engagement and addressed a challenge long experienced in informal and incidental learning—that is, the lack of corrective feedback in the moment. BOA matched newly emerging needs for different kinds of skilling with a variety of responses congruent with Ashby's (1991) Law of Requisite Variety. Technology opened the door to democratization and personalization of learning, putting choices about where, when, and how to learn in the hands of learners themselves—a recurring theme across many chapters.

Chapter 3 speaks to how L&D is rethinking responses to upskilling and reskilling, given the Future of Work, by sharing control and creating the conditions for "pull" versus "push." The vignettes in Chapter 3 leverage complexity dynamics demonstrating "how *small* moves, *smartly* made, can set *big* things in motion," the subtitle of *The Power of Pull* (Hagel III et al., 2010). Some organizations—Unilever (Chapter 3), but also PepsiCo (this chapter) and IBM (Chapter 2)—are developing talent from within their organizations to help employees reinvent career trajectories in light of the realization that half or more current jobs may disappear with consequent large-scale technological unemployment, even as new jobs are created.

Chapters 4 and 5 are based on work under way to rethink informal and incidental learning (IIL) in light of complexity science. Informal learning—typically organic and driven by the learner—depends for accuracy and richness on access to information in feedback loops that either amplify (positive) or dampen (negative) results of actions. Intelligent technologies can help learners become more aware of, and act on, feedback loops when they engage trial-and-trial learning and learning from error—that is, a mismatch between intentions and outcomes, as well as totally unintended consequences of which they may be unaware.

As Chapter 5 argues, the high velocity, interdependence, and non-linear nature of complex work elevates awareness of incidental learning. One senses, probes, responds, generates alternatives, and learns from experiences. Tacit knowing, incidentally acquired, helps to respond quickly to change and to generate creative ideas that live at the edges of our thinking. Incidental learning thrives through experimentation. "Creation spaces," a term introduced by Hagel III et al. (2010)—some self-managed, others facilitated; some in organized coursework, others in peer consultations on project work—help learners access, value, and use their tacit knowing when complexity demands it.

Chapter 6 is about our work on creating organizations with an enhanced capacity to learn. Our learning organization model consists of seven dimensions:

1. creating continuous learning opportunities
2. promoting dialogue and inquiry
3. encouraging collaboration and team learning
4. empowering people toward a collective vision
5. establishing systems to capture and share learning
6. making systemic connections with the environment
7. providing strategic leadership for learning

Research using our questionnaire, the *Dimensions of a Learning Organization Questionnaire* (DLOQ) demonstrates significant correlations with organizational performance, both financial and knowledge performance. The implications of this relationship offer strong support for the role of L&D in organizations. Recognizing the power of learning, the model also encourages considerable work with the culture to embed learning into the very DNA of the organization (Marsick & Watkins, 1999).

Chapter 7 draws on early work by Dechant et al. (1993) on learning while teaming. Teams need to learn collectively in order to innovate and advance their work. This chapter explores teaming as complex adaptive systems. Learning in complexity also requires new team processes. FlowTeams as described by Bill Gardner rethink group dynamics to create an organic knowledge producing approach that attempts to stir the abductive imagination. Finally, agile teams are adopted by many organizations.

Our studies of learning organization dimensions demonstrate that the most important dimension driving organizational performance is providing strategic leadership for learning (Watkins and Kim, 2018). Chapter 8 explores the role of leaders in promoting L&D, how their roles are becoming more distributed and shared, and how L&D can develop their capacity to work collectively.

Chapter 9 touches on a rapidly growing area of L&D—learning analytics—that has often been ignored, or focused only on learner satisfaction. How can data analytics be drawn upon to rethink L&D? Just because data are available does not mean they are meaningful in enhancing the work of L&D or in proving its worth.

By the end of this book, we hope you will better understand how the workplace L&D function is evolving in the midst of complexity. What new roles and missions are being enacted? Which potential future directions will be taken to meet the demands of a changing workforce? At the same time, we acknowledge that global upheaval brought on by the pandemic, political polarities, climate instability, and rapidly evolving technologies have made predictions of the future impossible. At the root of L&D work is learning and change. We explore our vision of workplace learning and development in the next chapter.

NOTE

1. *Complex* systems are different from complicated systems governed by Newtonian laws. Complex systems contain multiple components—usually many parts called agents. The more varied agents there are, the greater the strength and adaptability of the system. The components are interdependent—a change in one reverberates through *all* the others. Thus, the entire system is constantly in flux, evolving into new states, so it cannot be understood as a simple aggregation of its separate parts. Further, any intervention taken to mediate or measure the actions of any component of the system will inevitably change all system components.

   A complex system, then, can only be described in terms of the interactions among all its components. Trying to question which specific force(s) are determining the changing strength and path of a complex system like a hurricane with countless simultaneously interdependent factors, is impossible. For now, any answer(s) must remain in the realm of "Unknown Unknowns." Not just unknown—actually unknowable (North America Primary Care Research Group, downloaded from www.napcrg.org, n.d.).

   Complex systems can be organic, social, and material. Just a few examples: living cells, ants, a rainforest, the human brain, immune system, entire body; power, communication, or transportation grids; stock markets; medical departments and hospitals; workplace learning and development, social and economic organizations (like cities); ultimately the entire universe.

   Linked properties that characterize most, though not all, complex systems include adaptability, self-organization with distributed control, emergence, and unpredictability. Adaptability is their ability to alter operations and remain resilient over time, continuing to perform at a high level in the presence of changing environmental conditions. This property is so pervasive that the entire class are universally designated Complex Adaptive Systems—or CASs.

   When the system agents all begin to act in consonance with their local rules, their behavioral regularities emerge in an overall pattern characteristic of the CAS as a whole—one that typically demonstrates capabilities superior to any individual agent in the CAS. For example, a flock of birds reacts faster to a barrier or threat of a predator than could any individual bird. There is no one smarter or more agile bird directing the flock. If there were, centralized control would actually *slow down* the flock's capacity to react and adapt. Within complexity theory, emergence refers to this very specific process in which simple interactions among individual parts or agents form complex behaviors and patterns at the whole system level (Ladyman & Wiesner, 2020).

Unpredictability. Repetitive formation of precarious states occurs—via a process called "Self-Organized Criticality"—where just the tiniest addition or disturbance to a cone of sand or a wall of snow can cause an avalanche. Huge ones are rare, but the time and impetus for a *catastrophic* one is *completely unpredictable*. Thus, complexity can trigger a need for constant vigilance and awareness. Weick and Sutcliffe (2015, p. 69) appropriately observed: "You need to treat every ski slope as if you are riding it for the first time. The avalanche doesn't care about what you got away with last time."

2. Understanding workplace learning

Watkins' (1989) vision of human resource development and our definition of learning ground our vision of rethinking learning in the workplace in ways that meet complexity and other emerging demands on learners and organizations. This chapter lays out that vision and situates it in its broader fields.

THEORIES OF LEARNING

Learning has been illusive to define, although our understanding has benefitted from recent advances in neuroscience and cognitive science (National Academies of Sciences, Engineering, and Medicine, 2018). Most learning theories agree that learning is a change in something—a meaning scheme, behavior, skill, or knowledge. Where theories differ is in premises about how we learn and what that implies for learning redesign.

Early on, learning was conceptualized as what is written on the blank slate of our mind (Locke's *tabula rasa*). This assumes that something—presumably knowledge—is transmitted or observed and then retained. This approach was replaced by Pavlov's stimulus-response theory—a behaviorist theory of learning that centers on "*conditioning* [original italics], a nonconscious form of learning in which one automatically adjusts one's decisions and behaviors when particular and familiar contextual cues or triggers are present [and] can be strengthened when they are closely followed by rewards" (National Academies of Sciences, Engineering, and Medicine, 2018, p. 39). Over time, cognitive theories of learning emerged. Learning differs based on one's perspective on human cognition, as Fenwick (2000) aptly described. Kolb (1984), for example, emphasized cognitive constructivist dimensions of experiential learning as pushback to behaviorism. Recently, learning definitions add somatic dimensions involving metaphor, feelings, and affect (Taylor & Marienau, 2016).

Behaviorism dominates workplace learning, perhaps because performance requires skilling, and organizations need to motivate employees to meet externally imposed demands. Instructional designers often rely on ADDIE (Analyze, Design, Develop, Implement, Evaluate) and other formulaic behaviorist models that derive from a performance perspective (Swanson, 2022). These models have critics: for example, Bhattarai (2021) critiques the underlying behaviorist approach of train-the-trainer materials. Behaviorist models are effective when there are clear, right answers and best practices to be accurately replicated.

Complexity challenges these models. Alternatives arise, such as reliance on design thinking to innovate and experiment with alternatives. For example, SAM (Successive Approximation Model) uses rapid prototyping and an interactive process of building a course that "provides opportunities to experiment, test, and revise the designs. Development in small steps, with frequent evaluations, allows for changes that can be modified or reversed at a time when changes cost the least" (Jung et al., 2019, p. 193).

Learning delivery and its facilitation is being transformed by intelligent technology. So too are jobs and the way humans organize themselves for working. Theories of learning and of learning design focus on process. Definitions of learning look more closely at its outcomes.

DEFINING LEARNING

The *Oxford English Dictionary* offers definitions of learning as a noun,

> *n.* the acquisition of novel information, behaviors, or abilities after practice, observation, or other experiences, as evidenced by change in behavior, knowledge, or brain function. Learning involves consciously or nonconsciously attending to relevant aspects of incoming information, mentally organizing the information into a coherent cognitive representation, and integrating it with relevant existing knowledge activated from long-term memory.

and as a verb,

> to gain knowledge or skill by studying, from experience, from being taught, etc.[1]

Thus, the noun form of the word focuses on the outcome for the learner while the verb form focuses on the process. Learning can be consciously or nonconsciously acquired—distinctions key to rethinking L&D today.

The degree of conscious awareness of learning something new differentiates among formal, informal, and incidental learning. Bransford et al. (2005) identify three perspectives on learning: the behaviorist that sees learning as a strengthening of associations between stimuli and responses; the constructivist that views learning as the growth of conceptual structures and of reasoning and problem-solving ability; and the situative that views learning as tied to social interaction and cultural tools. They point to pattern recognition by which a stimulus is matched with information stored in memory that yields identification of patterns. Pattern recognition is central to machine and artificial intelligence learning. It is also key to informal and incidental learning. Reber, a cognitive scientist, described implicit learning—often used synonymously with incidental learning—as an underlying process of "rapid, effortless, and untutored detection of patterns of co-variation among events in the world" (1993, p. 5). While views differ as to how this happens, there is no doubt that it happens.

Distinction between formal and informal learning, according to Bransford et al. (2005), "marks some rough differences between self-organized, emergent learning and learning occasioned by organized instruction and designed curricula" (p. 40). Yet, they note that context-based definitions of formal and informal learning fall apart since either schooling or non-school contexts may have the same properties. "If we set aside the firm distinction between 'informal' and 'formal' the foundational issue becomes the structuring properties of contexts for learning and development" (p. 40). Who decides and how learning is structured become defining characteristics more than the context.

Thus, an integrative definition of learning as a verb pulls from several learning theorists. Learning is,

> the way in which individuals or groups acquire, interpret, reorganize, change or assimilate a related cluster of information, skills and feelings. It is also primary to the way in which people construct meaning in their personal and shared organizational lives. (Marsick, 1987, p. 4)

Brown and Thomas (2009) extend Brown's earlier work on situated learning. They believe that what is needed in the 21st century is learning to become—over and over again (p. 321). They note, "In a world of flux, knowing, making, and playing emerge as critical components of becoming" (p. 324). Play enables participants to co-construct and re-construct the context as well as the situation through engaging the imagination (p. 327). Through pragmatic imagination, context "is continually changing and being remade with each act of participation. These communities of becoming themselves are rich constructs that fuse notions of interest, technological infrastructure, and co–presence (often in the form of joint work) into the idea of a 'networked imagination'" (Brown & Thomas, 2009, p. 324). The authors conclude that, amidst "infinite complexity, endless possibility, and near constant change … our approach to education and learning needs to be as rich and complex as the challenges and opportunities we face" (p. 335).

Our Perspective on Learning

Our view of learning grows out of a social-constructivist lens that centers on meaning making in interaction with others (Marsick, 1987). Over time we moved to situational and enactivist lenses as organizational life became more complex. We saw that people learn and construct meaning at work through interaction with others and with the tools of the situation. We edged toward enactivist learning, described by Fenwick (2000) as evolving simultaneously through experiential learning as co-evolution of cognition and the environment in the context of networked ecologies. As Justice et al. (2020) argue, learning in dynamical contexts depends on interdependent relationships. They draw on, the idea, as Colombetti and Thompson (2007) explain, that the

> "human mind is embodied in our entire organism and embedded in the world, and hence not reducible to structures inside the head. Meaning and experience are created by, or enacted through, the continuous reciprocal interaction of the brain, the body, and the world." (Justice et al., 2020, p. 324)

Thus individuals are interdependent with complex systems through frequently changing, entangled relationships.

Drawing as we do on experiential learning, with roots in Dewey (1938) and Lewin (1947), we conceptualize workplace learning as frequently informal, shaped by context, often focused on solving problems within one's work, and evolving through collaborative action and reflection (Marsick & Watkins, 1990/2015). We do not exclude formal learning, but it typically is also prompted by, applied to, or otherwise linked with work. We recognize that learning is often collaborative and social. It is embedded in organizational communities. We take an organization development perspective that argues for a learning-rich culture, scaffolded to promote and support learning within complexity.

Human Resource Development

Watkins (1989) defined human resource development (HRD) as,

> the field of study and practice responsible for the fostering of a long-term, work-related learning capacity at the individual, group, and organizational level of organizations. As such, it includes—but is not limited to—training, career development, and organizational development. (p. 427)

From this perspective, the function of the learning and organization development unit(s) is clear—that is, change the capacity of individuals, groups, and the organization to fulfill its purpose in the long term. We see this vision as leading quite clearly to creating a learning organization (Watkins & Marsick, 1993).

How do we change capacity? At the individual level, increased capacity is the ability to do something greater than what one has done to date. Unleashed capacity refers to those capabilities the organization has identified, but not yet applied. For example, IBM once discovered that many employees knew foreign languages that could enable them to work in other countries. This language capacity was an untapped resource IBM could draw on when entering a new market. Individuals engage informal learning to solve problems and complete new projects. Individuals' willingness to learn in order to work more effectively and their motivation to find new solutions to stubborn problems are a great asset to an organization. The response of workers to the pandemic globally—for example, to learn how to work remotely and adapt to the myriad interruptions, closures, sickness, and other challenges that characterized this period—testify to both individuals' willingness to learn and the organizational importance of this hidden capacity. Context is a singular feature of informal and incidental learning (Ellinger & Cseh, 2007). It influences how people learn in different situations and speaks to how underlying principles need to be adapted.

At the unit level, capacity is enhanced when the group acquires new skills, develops new products, etc. Design thinking, maker spaces (communal project working spaces), and collaborative creativity allow teams to bring new products and processes to market more rapidly. For example, *agile* is a collaborative group process that enhances capacity by accelerating the launch of new products through iterative development in self-organizing teams. People develop learning and teamwork capacities they can additionally use going forward.

When the organization as a whole adds a new capacity—for example, introducing a successful new product or opening a market—it adds potential long-term strength. In our work, the key to rethinking L&D for capacity building is creating a learning culture. We identified seven dimensions of a learning organization that are significant to developing organizational capacity at all levels and that enhance organizational knowledge performance. The seven dimensions are interdependent. Actions, and their consequences, ripple through groups and individuals connected to the work being done—throughout a group, across boundaries in the organization, and often through an ecosystem of organizations networked together in mutually beneficial ways.

UNDERSTANDING LEARNING IN THE WORKPLACE

Learning in the workplace is not unlike learning in any other setting—when someone learns, something changes—knowledge, a skill, an attitude, a perspective. So what difference does the workplace context make? Employee learning is shaped by employers to meet their goals and objectives. Learning in the industrial era was centered on training for best practices, and standardized ways of working. In the post-industrial era, learning is adaptive, often initiated and directed by learners, knowledge-centered, and innovative. Employers seek to influence outcomes, and shape learning they directly provide, but they do not control many of the learners' choices.

Lundgren and Poell (2020) call attention to differences in the role of workplace learning, reflected in a tension between "learning versus performance" (p. 277). Which of the two should HRD emphasize? In this regard, Swanson (2022) focuses on the assumptions each paradigm makes about the purpose of the L&D function. Performance perspectives assume that when an individual produces more of what is expected, or does it better, the organization will automatically have better results. We know, however, that this is not necessarily the case. Other changes, such as those facilitated by organization developers, may be needed to translate individual performance gains into organizational benefits.

Learning may be an intrinsic part of solving a problem, or it can be autonomously self-initiated, or even mandated by someone else, perhaps as part of a performance review. Instructional designers or facilitators might structure learning as part of formal training programs; but increasingly, this may be left to the individual to figure out. Learners may access online programs or search the internet for information on the topic, or they may tap into their social network. Who can they email or otherwise talk with who has knowledge about this problem? In other words, as George Siemens (2004) asks in connectivism theory, what knowledge can we draw upon from our personal learning network?

Kuchinke (1998) writes, "whatever the flavor of the HRD intervention, whether it be training, employee wellness, culture change, or transfer of expertise, its ultimate value is the degree to which it can contribute to the company's overarching purpose" (p. 379). Jacobs and Park (2009) echo Kuchinke's focus on organizational needs:

> We define workplace learning as the process used by individuals when engaged in training programs, education and development courses, or some type of experiential learning activity for the purpose of acquiring the competence necessary to meet current and future work requirements. The definition assumes the need to balance, though not always equally, the needs of organizations, which provide the context for the learning, with the needs of individuals who may undertake the learning to advance their own work-related interests and goals. (Jacobs & Park, 2009, p. 134)

Jacobs and Park's conceptualization of workplace learning focuses on the variations among three major variables: the degree of planning (from unstructured to structured), the location of learning (on or off the job), and the role of others (is the learner active or passive in the process?).

The L&D Function

How, then, is L&D situated and supported in organizations? The Chartered Institute for Professional Development (CIPD) in England and the Association for Talent Development (ATD) in the United States are the two major professional associations for practitioners in this field. Both offer courses and certification in the field and publish myriad materials targeted to practitioners in the various areas of practice associated with the L&D function. CIPD (n.d.)[2] defines learning and development thus:

> Learning and development is about creating the right culture and environment for individuals and organisations to learn and grow. It's knowing the current and future capability needs of the organisation, as well as how to create a learning culture that drives engagement in ongoing professional development.

Learning design and delivery requires a blend of learning approaches … as well as the application of motivational and behavioural science. How effectively learning is transferred to the learner is key to understanding its impact.[3]

This definition aligns well with our conception of the L&D function. It consists of all of those activities that focus on learning and growth—and that build organizational capability. Ultimately its goal is to create a culture focused on learning—that should be measured not only by its impact on individual learners but also on the organization.

The Association for Talent Development (ATD, n.d.) states:

> Learning and development (L&D) is a function within an organization that is responsible for empowering employees' growth and developing their knowledge, skills, and capabilities to drive better business performance ….
>
> The term, learning and development, encompasses any professional development a business provides to its employees. It … may sometimes be referred to as training and development, learning and performance, or talent development (TD).[4]

This functional conception emphasizes enhanced business performance. Professional associations' understanding of workplace learning continues to evolve as practice evolves. A forerunner in evolving conceptions of workplace learning is IBM. We look now at how IBM is rethinking learning and development.

BOX 2.1 RETHINKING L&D AT IBM

Gordon Fuller, Vice President and Chief Learning Officer

Seven or eight years ago, we were thinking about how we can make learning not just attractive and engaging for learners, but also vital to individuals. We looked at how we were deploying learning and the traditional management learning system we were using, which has been built to benefit the process owners and administrators. It is not designed for a satisfying learner experience. We found that 90% of the learning consumed by IBMers was from outside IBM!

We rethought our delivery using the principles of design thinking. You look at the business outcome first, and then you make it completely user-centric, engaging. You iterate all the time. We used the principles of Agile. We worked in sprints; and had literally thousands of sponsor users, over 400 key user groups who looked at our latest iterations and gave feedback: "That looks good. Is it possible to do this? What if we did that?"

We had an idea of what we wanted, but we used the principle of "offer management," not product management, in order to keep focused on the customer and not our idea about the product. (Laura Fay, Technology & Services Industry Association, explains that Technology Product Managers innovate by creating compelling user experiences, whereas Offer Managers innovate with differentiated value propositions to grow overall market share.) We wanted to develop a platform that was truly "blue sky" and virgin territory. In the end, we built what might be the "truly first learner experience platform!" And we did it with no major stakeholders other than users—and with no budget. We built in the mornings, lunchtimes, evenings, weekends—it was basically what you call a "skunkworks."

Six or seven months before we launched, we shared it with experts and a few key stakeholders. We could make further enhancements because we kept the agile two-week sprints going all these years. We still work in iterations and tweaks to the program. And looking at it today by comparison to the original, it's night and day.

It wasn't a big launch. We had about 2,500–3,000 advocates before we started, so we gave them the first links to the tool. As they had a part in the design, they sent it to all their friends in IBM, who liked what they could do with it and sent it out to their friends. Within three months we had over 96% of IBM using it. It is still the most used application in IBM.

Change Made in L&D

So what did it accomplish? And this is where the change in L&D comes! L&D has traditionally been about taking courses, passing tests, and receiving a badge or certificate. And then we make them a little bit better at this or that. But the half-life of skills is getting shorter and shorter every few years; and the Social Security safety net is gradually being withdrawn by mature governments around the world. If you consider advances in Artificial Intelligence and healthcare, people are generally living longer—that is, if we don't blow up the planet, ruin it with climate change, or suffer another pandemic. So the new college graduates might see no reason to think that they will be flipping burgers if they rely on their degree alone to get them through their working life. The only way they can advance—by sheer necessity, just to survive, just to be counted—is to become a continuous learner. I wanted to create a social contract of transparency in terms of helping employees get skills they need for the future. They see newspaper articles about how their company is letting go of people who no longer have the skill sets needed, and at the same time hiring younger people with new skills. I wanted to help people learn new skills so they could advance in the company and IBM could retain and develop their talents.

I am a big fan of Dan Pink's idea of motivation 3.0. He says that one of the first things you do is to give people autonomy and ownership. I did not forget that 90% of learning was getting consumed outside of trusted internal sources—some paid, some completely free. I wanted employees to think when they came into this platform: "I have autonomy here because I can search for anything."

The new system needed to say: "You're a software architect right now, but you want to be a back-end quantum developer at some point. Here are the roles and skills coming at you over the horizon. Click the boxes, add other areas you'd like to learn—Agile, containers, or whatever. Check all these boxes, press 'save.'" And the magic that happens is that the platform will recognize you because it has trusted source connectors to all these internal and external resources—the most critically important of these connectors being to the Human Resource Information Warehouse. So, from the first time an employee enters, it knows them, knows their job, knows their tenure with the company, which business they're in, what they need to know to do their current job better. The next time they go in, there's a different interface with recommendations tailored to them, e.g.: "You know this, but you aspire to that. Here are some of the things you should be looking at." And you get to choose what method or media you use to learn: Do you want videos? Face-to-face? Self-learning or coaching, mentoring, whatever. It will build a learning plan. You're in Job A and aspire to Job B. This is what you have to do. This is your learning plan. And what it will also say, for example, is that there are ten modules in this plan. And maybe you already know the material in some modules or used these skills in another job. So, we test them to verify that they know material in some number of modules. That does two things. One, it truncates the time to capability. And two, it decreases the potential for user frustration.

So that gave us autonomy. I also focused on the second part of motivation 3.0, which is "mastery." Mastery is not passing exams; it's demonstrating skills. We built a very powerful digital nudging capability based on the work of Richard Thaler. Not only do we identify what people want to do and give them a learning plan; we also monitor how they get through it. Not to be Big Brother, but we can say: "Hey, Gordon, you're doing great, you're about 45% of the way through this. And we have found that people who are good at this are normally about 60% of the way through. Let's just have a look at these next two programs coming up and get you back on track." So, we get them quickly to mastery!

The last step to motivation 3.0 is a sense of purpose. I help the people who go through this rapid learning and development skills building to get jobs—that's the latest thing we started to do. And then I use them as faculty members in my skills academies. They give back! "Somebody got me here, and I can pass it on as subject matter expert." It's a technique that is as old as the hills: If you want to reinforce learning, you get people to teach it.

Impact

So let's go to career velocity. In 2013, then CEO Ginni Rometty issued a challenge to the IBM workforce: "I would like you to commit to 40 hours of personal development learning in a year." And you could hear the corporate sharp intake of breath: "Here I am, working my head off. I can watch TV five hours a night and I can play golf all day Saturday. But where am I going to find 40 hours a year to learn?" But they did it. The average hours per learner in IBM last year was 88! And many people regularly exceed that.

We came back to this digital nudging. We decided to recognize people who are achieving at high levels. Table stakes is, "Think 40 hours." Super learners are anybody above last year's average. There are no foundation badges in IBM, only skills badges. There are three categories of super learners based in part on these badges: bronze at 120 hours plus one skills badge; silver at 160 hours plus two skills badges; gold at 200 plus three skill badges. We're leveraging not only digital nudging, but also socialization and gamification. We have something called a "framer." So the recognition as a super learner, with the year and level achieved, is added to your profile picture in IBM as a frame. People put this on LinkedIn! And they get a competition going within learning cohorts.

But it's not just about getting framed. Skills development leads to performance and career development. If I look at the top 20% of learners in IBM compared to the bottom 20%, they have 26% greater career velocity, they get 22% more promotions, 16% more increases in compensation. An interesting data point is that they also have an 8% greater propensity to leave the company. And because we know they have this propensity to leave, we can start applying positive retention techniques right away. Many times, learning is the retention tool because they are getting their career developed at IBM. What's the number one thing that new graduates want in jobs? They don't want employment, they want employability. Who's going to give me street cred! And the experience and the infrastructure to advance and develop.

We demonstrate value. Our analysis says that L&D does contribute to the greater sum of revenue growth, free cash flow, as well as diversity and inclusion inside IBM—which are three big drivers! It leads us to command the key domains, get increased wallet share, and cloud AI cybersecurity and quantum. If we can't engage our own people, we will struggle to engage our learners. How can we make this a mission, and not just a job!

The biggest shift in adopting this approach is not in the technology, it's in the mindset. There are learning platforms everywhere, but we need to make sure that we design it for the user, for the learner, not just to support our processes and workstreams. So the first thing is to change the mindset. That means listening to the learner, working with the learner, and not doing it for them, but doing it with them. If they *are not* part of the process, why would they accept it? Whereas if they *are* part of the solution, you bet your bottom dollar that they're going to be telling everybody about it. You create advocates! You not only get the best insight into what creates the best platform. You also get the people who are going to go out and promote it for you.

People ask, "What's your key metric?", and expect me to say learning hours per user or number of people with skills badges. But that's not it. It's how many people have I placed in jobs inside IBM—new jobs, different jobs? We have this organization called Internal Career Mobility. I've got these skills academies. They deepen skills, get new certifications, new skills badges. I get subject matter experts who then become faculty members. What I want to do now—it is not off the ground yet—is to build job centers in the skills academies. I don't want to wait until people have graduated to find them new jobs in IBM. Before they graduate, I want to get potential managers and recruiters to say we're looking for this, or for that. Find a way to connect these future graduates with new opportunities.

So, my metric is how many people have I moved into new jobs that saved IBM from going out and buying 5,000 newbies? We've got to be superfine about who we bring into the company, but what a waste of potential if we ignore and don't develop the talent and skills of the 5,000 people already inside the company who are 10% away from doing it, have proved loyal to the company, have an internal network, and have other skills that will be useful.

When we first designed this new approach to L&D, I described this expression: the triumvirate of responsibility. There are three parts, three owners. One is the committed learner, somebody who is not here just to tread water, who genuinely wants to learn, advance, develop. Second is that the organization provides a good learning experience platform that lets them search, get personalized recommendations, knows them and allows them to change the profile, the skills path, provides assistance in learning paths, testing and assessment. But the third and last one, that often gets overlooked, is the role of the manager. The manager is actively involved and taking responsibility for the person's development. We're building a three-legged stool, and you can't leave off any one of those three legs.

The IBM skilling stories illustrate a focus on skilling and creation of new learning designs. Additionally, as we will see in other chapters, Fuller innovated by creating a learner-centric process. Technology is a partner, helping L&D become more customized and personalized, and yet at a scale hitherto impossible. We explore the future of work and illustrate the role of technology in reshaping learning in the next chapter.

NOTES

1. https://www.oed.com (accessed March 16, 2023).
2. https://peopleprofession.cipd.org/profession-map/specialist-knowledge/learning-development#gref (accessed March 16, 2023).
3. https://peopleprofession.cipd.org/profession-map/specialist-knowledge/learning-development#gref (accessed March 16, 2023).
4. https://www.td.org/talent-development-glossary-terms/what-is-learning-and-development, n.d. (accessed October 6, 2022).

3. Exploring future trends in L&D

Many reports and articles identify technology as a dominant trend transforming how learning is delivered, with implications for trends of skilling and the future of work.

Technological tools have propelled the pivot to digital delivery and created whole new possibilities. The Fourth Industrial Revolution (Hofmann & Rüsch, 2017) has changed the nature of products, services, and work practices/processes. Technology is vital to new skills needed to partner with automation and Artificial Intelligence (AI). It affects the speed of work and expands the network of people engaged in transactions across geographic boundaries and cross-boundary ecosystems. What will the metaverse enable? Already, virtual reality (VR) simulations allow more authentic experiences for such disparate things as learning to be a pilot or performing surgery.

Lyle Yorks looks at how AI, VR, and other technologies are being used to support learning and development at Bank of America (BOA).

BOX 3.1 THE ACADEMY AT BANK OF AMERICA: ENHANCING PERFORMANCE AND TALENT MANAGEMENT THROUGH THE APPLICATION OF AI FOR LEARNING AND DEVELOPMENT

Lyle Yorks, Ed.D., Professor Emeritus, Teachers College, Columbia University & Distinguished Principal Research Fellow, The Conference Board

Jennifer R. Burnett, Ph.D., Principal, Human Capital, The Conference Board

Driven in part by the increasingly rapid pace of advances in technology, regardless of industry, organizations are confronting significant talent management challenges. These include a need for reskilling and upskilling the workforce as technological innovation around intelligent digital technologies goes beyond automating aspects of work to assisting and augmenting employees as they perform their tasks. This need for enhanced learning and development practices is increased by having to anticipate and respond to the skill gaps that will exist in the near future as both organizational strategy changes and technological innovations continue. At the same time, businesses are confronting talent acquisition and talent retention challenges as the labor market becomes more agile. Providing an effective onboarding experience to new employees that gets them prepared for doing their jobs is important for both employee performance and retention.

Developing The Academy at Bank of America

Bank of America has always had a large learning function within its Global Human Resources organization. In 2017, Bank of America's Consumer Line of Business built out additional training and coaching capabilities in what they called "Consumer Academy" (The Academy) under the leadership of John Jordan. The concept of The Academy originated when John was asked by Dean Athanasia (President of Regional Banking) to work with a large team to build an organization partnering with HR teammates to strategically address key talent management issues, specifically onboarding and retention, faced in the consumer bank. Eventually The Academy organization grew to support other client-facing businesses and was consolidated under the Human Resources umbrella as the global learning and skills development organization for the Bank.

Since The Academy's founding, John Jordan's focus has been listening to the needs expressed by employees as they go through the onboarding process. A significant point that emerged from employee feedback was, "We want practice routes beyond reading, clicking through training materials and relying on facilitators when doing role-plays." Beyond knowing about recommended actions, they wanted to experience the process of putting their responsibilities into action, building the skills and capabilities for performance as they engaged with clients regarding their bank accounts while using various systems to service them. These were front-line employees who were interacting with clients regarding opening accounts, servicing their accounts, resolving issues, and answering questions while working with technology systems to address the issues. They wanted to practice real-world scenarios to effectively provide their services, while also strengthening their relationship with clients. The use of technology to simulate client interactions through a virtual environment emerged as a central part of the learner experience for delivering this learning along with coaching from experienced business professionals. The learning staff coaching the learning process were brought into The Academy from various businesses across the organization. They understood the learning goals and content and could provide feedback from a practitioner perspective. Consistent with this focus on the needs expressed by the learners, following completion of a module or program the central assessment question asked of the learners is: "Do you feel prepared for the job?"

The Academy provides specific courses that new hires complete for their onboarding process. From its inception, providing a positive onboarding process that made new hires comfortable with their job and aware of the potential for continuing their development was the intention of The Academy. Research has documented that the onboarding experience has a significant impact on employee retention. John repeatedly makes the point that if a new employee has a poor onboarding experience, they are more likely to leave the company in the first six months to a year. In addition, courses are available for employees to enroll in to further develop their skills.

Application of Technologies

The answers employees provided regarding what they wanted from their learning experiences were addressed through the application of technologies that simulated practice. Three examples of these technologies are:

1. *Academy Client Engagement Simulators (ACES)*: These simulations put the employees in a particular work situation in which they must work through a specific type of problem or service opportunity. They can continue to practice incorporating feedback from coaching based on their earlier response. One-on-one coaching can be provided. The Academy provides specific courses that new hires complete as part of their onboarding process. As described above, from its inception, providing a positive onboarding process that made new hires comfortable with their job and aware of the potential for their continuing development was the intention of The Academy. Role-specific simulations for onboarding and coaching are provided through The Academy, using more than a hundred different simulations to practice a wide range of skills. In addition to specific courses, employees can sign in to use simulations to practice and improve their skills.
2. *iCoach*: An on-demand platform powered by artificial intelligence that allows for interactive coaching. Learners interact with iCoach to receive on-the-spot, interactive coaching, as well as recommendations on targeted scenarios, helping teammates develop new skills quickly. AI acts like a client to simulate the conversation and will also correct the learner through feedback provided in real-time. Learners can practice a conversation over and over until they have achieved mastery.
3. *Virtual Reality*: Simulations that provide teammates with an immersive coaching tool on the "moments that matter." The learner is placed holistically in a client call or interaction that plays out through the scenario. Over a dozen VR applications have been created for financial

center employees and Merrill, the Investment Management and Wealth Management division of the bank, to provide lifelike client interactions and decision making on-demand. VR is useful for developing soft skills like empathy. For example, one module in particular provides experience taking calls from clients who are experiencing a personally difficult situation such as the loss of a loved one.

The Academy contributes to:

- higher productivity on the part of employees
- a decrease in employees leaving the organization
- an increase in career mobility of employees across the organization
- a reduction in error rates

The Broader Range of Learner Development

Human–machine interaction is central to the learning process at The Academy. It is also integrated into the talent management process. As mentioned above, The Academy has merged as a corporate function under HR. It has become part of the career development process as the technologies used also enable certifying the learning taking place. Career development is enabled through employees being able to map how their skills interconnect with roles in various career path options. This has influenced career mobility as more than 50 percent of new hires in various business units are internal to Bank of America. The use of these technologies has provided more confidence in employees for moving from one business unit of the bank to another because they know they will be given support through The Academy; they'll have resources such as coaches and be provided practice simulations. The level of engagement of employees with the bank has increased, as reflected in lower numbers of employees leaving the bank. A culture of agility and career development has been strengthened at a time when a skills-based approach to enhancing talent mobility is becoming increasingly important.

As the applications of intelligent technologies with a focus on simulating situations for practice are being used across the HR talent management process, from talent acquisition to career mobility, The Academy has also provided opportunities for building relationships with underserved, low-to-moderate income communities, building a more diverse workforce. One no longer needs a college degree to apply for front-line jobs at Bank of America. Once the applicants are hired, The Academy provides the resources for learning the skills necessary to be good at the job. Resources are also provided for the employees to pursue a degree if they want to. The Academy works with community colleges and non-profits through the bank's Pathways programs. By investing in technology, the organizations' people infrastructure, and listening to what people say they need to learn to be successful, The Academy reduces entry barriers and provides the learning experiences people need.

The Academy supplements the bank's enterprise programs, focused on manager development, through specific programs for managing a financial center or being a local market leader. These programs get much more into the technical aspects of the job. Virtual reality is provided for managers to practice conducting difficult conversations, like coaching conversations. One of the additional benefits for managers is freeing up the capacity of their workforce. Now they know that when they send someone to a program, they will be much more proficient when they complete the program. If someone needs a refresher because they have been away or doing other tasks, they can take the training and come back capable of performing. Protected time may be available through The Academy to allow for this reskilling.

Summary

As learning has become an important aspect of talent management practices, it needs to be integrated into an overall human capital development strategy. The Academy is a high impact pillar within the talent management process. Talent acquisition finds strong talent for the company and resources are provided by The Academy, educating the acquired talent to effectively perform their job through the onboarding process and beyond. A feedback loop exists between the two functions. The Academy provides ongoing learning and professional development opportunities for career development, and onboarding for new roles when employees move to a new role or job within the company. The Academy also provides managers with resources for addressing the learning needs of their employees. As the use of intelligent simulation technologies allows The Academy staff to track and certify the skills demonstrated by the learners in the simulations, managers know what their employees have learned and can do based on demonstrated performance. The Academy is also an asset for the company's commitment to diversity & inclusion. All this is possible because technology professionals in the company who create and adapt these simulations are familiar with underlying experiential learning theories, and learning and development professionals are conversant with technologies. They are a team working together, not separated functions.

BOA has drawn on new technologies to enhance learning and development and provide highly individualized development at scale. This capacity to do more in increasingly differentiated ways matches the complexity of learners' needs. Ashby's Law of Requisite Variety (Ashby, 1991) for the control of complex systems identifies the need to match variety in the system with an equal variety of responses. Technology is helping L&D do that. However, these changes are not without cost.

FUTURE OF WORK—THE SKILLS REVOLUTION

Schwab and Malleret (2020) posited that the pandemic triggered a "great reset":

> Nothing will ever return to the "broken" sense of normalcy that prevailed prior to the crisis because the coronavirus pandemic marks a fundamental inflection point in our global trajectory. ... We will continue to be surprised by both the rapidity and unexpected nature of these changes—as they conflate with each other, they will provoke second-, third-, fourth- and more-order consequences, cascading effects and unforeseen outcomes. In so doing, they will shape a "new normal" radically different from the one we will be progressively leaving behind. Many of our beliefs and assumptions about what the world could or should look like will be shattered in the process. (p. 8)

This reset affects multiple aspects of society—beginning with the economy. Three key forces are shaping the world today: interdependence, velocity, and complexity (Schwab & Malleret, 2020, p. 13). These forces also affect learning and development. Interdependence feeds increasing reliance on networks, communities of practice, and collective approaches. Velocity shortens time for learning, for example, emphasizing micro-learning, learning in the flow of work, and online resources. Complexity is ubiquitous. Schwab and Malleret (2020) note that the degree of complexity is determined by three factors:

> 1) the amount of information content or the number of components in a system; 2) the interconnectedness—defined as the dynamic of reciprocal responsiveness—between these pieces of information or components; and 3) the effect of non-linearity (... often called "tipping points"). Non-linearity is a key feature of complexity because it means that a change in just one component of a system can lead to a surprising and disproportionate effect elsewhere. (p. 18)

These elements—an information and data deluge, interconnectedness, and non-linearity—affect the learning and development function as surely as they do the rest of society.

Schwab (2017) explored potential changes to the nature of work as part of the Fourth Industrial Revolution. This digital revolution blurs the lines between the physical, digital, and biological. It could lead to the loss of up to half or more of current jobs, and to large-scale technological unemployment. It is creating new jobs at increasing rates. At a minimum, it calls for massive reskilling and upskilling. As well, many will have to adjust to, and hopefully learn to live, without work. Frey and Osborne (2013, p. 45) explained that industrial-era technology disruptions largely simplified tasks. Intelligent technologies, by contrast, call for deeper, sometimes cross-boundary, learning, as well as partnered learning between humans and machines. They further observed that "the reason why human labour has prevailed relates to its ability to acquire new skills. Yet this will become increasingly challenging as new work requires a higher degree of cognitive abilities" (Frey & Osborne, 2015, p. 89). How can humans develop these cognitive skills? Learning depends on the opportunities and resources in one's environment, whether formal or informal. How can gaps be closed between haves and have-nots? Frey and Osborne note that access is made all the more difficult by the rising costs of education. Moreover, how can education at all levels be transformed to center learning in a digital world?

In the vignette below, Ahreum Lim brings a critical look at some of the less obvious implications of the current discourse about the future of work.

BOX 3.2 TRACING THE FUTURE OF WORK DISCOURSE

Ahreum Lim, The University of Georgia

Active discourse concerning the future of work arose in the early 20th century, prompted by the emergence of industrial capitalism based on machine-mediated mass production (Crawford, 2021). The machine industrial era introduced automation of production via sequential use of tools by groups of workers on the factory floor. While the machine–worker relationship was initially collaborative, as practice evolved over time with improvements in both mechanics and worker performance, an element of competition between men and machines regarding value of output arose concomitantly. This competition has persisted in large-scale work up to and including the present time. The human implications have led to the intertwining of both psychological and socio-political considerations in ongoing commentaries on the meaning and nature of work, which is not infrequently portrayed as alienating or exploitative from Heideggerian or Marxist perspectives.

During the Industrial Revolution, human labor became exchanged in a specifically time-related way; a laborer's time became a segmented currency, compartmentalized into units of time that could be bought, sold, and exchanged (Crawford, 2021). In a way similar to that which occurred in mass production, management decision making—that formerly solely involved human agency—is increasingly segmented and managed by algorithms, or technical tools (Dastin, 2018; Rosenblat, 2018).

Historically, the future of work has gained particular attention since World War II, which produced intensifying, even urgent, demands for the increases in productivity—hence, automation. Work discourse has expanded since the 1950s. Figure 3.2.1, below, shows variations in emphasis since 1945 of the phrase "future of work" in Google N-gram search.

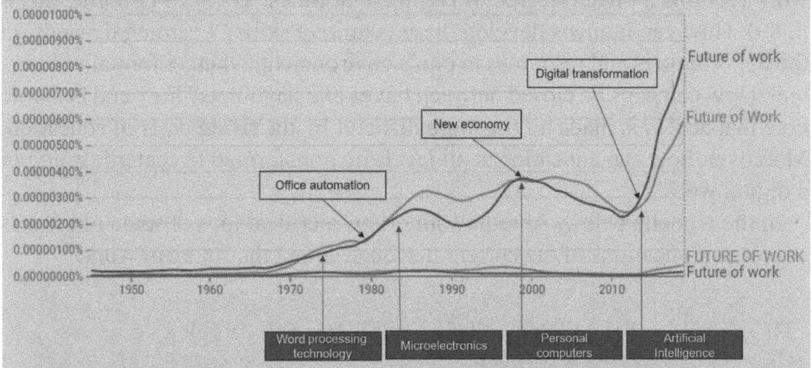

Figure 3.2.1 Google N-gram search marked with material and discursive development

The figure shows three peaks of the discourse: in the mid-1980s, the near 2000s, and after 2010. Not surprisingly peaks representing periods of preponderance coincide with discrete technologic advances in capacity to do large-scale work.

In the mid-1980s, the production niche was word-processing technology that was expected to help assign all typing and transcription jobs to specialists (Haigh, 2006). Then, in the near 2000s, the rapid development of the microprocessor and the availability of stand-alone computers allowed for the expansion of multinational corporations and globalization (Smith, 2001). The third peak of discourse emerges out of the invention of smart technology, sophisticated algorithms, artificial intelligence, automation, and robotics (Rosenblat, 2018, Stiegler, 2016).

In a little more detail, in the mid-1980s, the introduction of word-processing technology brought about a reorganization of the way labor was assigned to secretaries, eliminating arduous stenographic work—typing and transcribing. In turn, harsh cultural resistance emerged from clerical workers, with reported feelings of alienation due to the mechanization of their labor (Glenn and Feldberg, 1977). The introduction of microelectronics led to the invention of management information system (MIS) which indexed, stored, and retrieved human performance as data. This reinforced the hierarchical bureaucracy within the organization, creating or increasing a disparity between managers and workers (Nichols & Beynon, 1977). Despite the increased prominence of female laborers in the workplace, women were concentrated in traditional positions with fewer financial rewards and purviews compared to males (Baran, 1987).

The advent of telecommunications technology yielded hopeful speculation of a globalized New Economy, on top of speculations about further increases in efficiency. A "networked office automation" (Haigh, 2006, p. 26) became imaginable, with the sophistication of intelligent text processing and visualization technology implemented with a user-friendly interface. The accelerated wave of globalization after the collapse of the Soviet Union in 1989 also contributed further to a rosy picture of the future of work. A whole new global world order was imagined, with hypothetical social organizations supposedly promoting democratization, humanization, and continuing modernization (Beck, 2000). Smith (2001), through his study of companies in different industries, determined that the macro-level changes embedded in globalization triggered organizational interest in newly flexible management. The profusion of rosy pictures of a globalized, New/Knowledge Economy was criticized socio-politically as a way of subsuming, i.e., subordinating, human value in a logic of marketization (i.e., Fairclough, 2003).

Now, with the advent of new technologies, including more—even vastly—advanced computational intelligence, the response to the changes is seriously bifurcated. On the negative side, most are fearful of the 24/7 surveilling forces made possible through the application of increasingly economically attainable visual information technology. Some believe disembodied intelligence to be the most objective, bias-free, and lacking errors. Broussard (2018) forcefully criticized this projection as techno-chauvinistic dogma delegating the authority of decision making to a centralized, computational intelligence. By contrast, rosy sunrise adherents hold such a critical perspective to be too dismissive of the promised land that is projected to lie ahead of us—one in which computational algorithms can be fully autonomous, relieving us of any need to worry about obligatory tasks (Danaher, 2019).

The historical understanding of the future of work seen through a socio-technical lens sheds light on the unique role of learning in worker development. In the 1970s, learning (via training) was emphasized, particularly for clerical workers who were required to use new word-processing technology. However, at higher organizational levels, some empirical studies confirmed that this process also could lead to deskilling, as routinized tasks were assigned to machines, causing a stratification of human labor. Technological advancement was beneficial for skilled, highly-educated, often male, managers where training or, particularly, self-directed learning became increasingly necessary to keep up with changes in the area of practice (Glenn & Feldberg, 1977). The role of learning in development gained the utmost prominence with globalization as knowledge became a key intangible asset for individuals as well as companies (Barley, 1996). Knowledge workers came further to the forefront, and reskilling of individuals via personal learning became more urgent as the value half-life of useful—even sometimes proprietary—organizational knowledge and work practices progressively declined (Smith, 2001). Expansion of this trend, accompanied by parallel increases in automation, also threatened job displacement, competition directing knowledge workers onto an unceasing treadmill of learning, relearning … and relearning. Further, the modern lack of loyal company–worker relations, as well as competition from other employers, promoted frequent employee moves from company to company. This required near-relentless adaptation to new contexts, as well as anxiety about replacement by more powerfully automated "machines"—potentially also giving rise to dissociation and Marxian Alienation. In sum, projections concerning the future of work became less well founded … and increasingly dark.

Whether automation is leading to rich new jobs or creating worker alienation, the rapidity of these changes has created demands for upskilling, new skilling, and reskilling. L&D is helping workers respond.

THE SKILLS REVOLUTION

Demand for new skills has grown at the same time the global labor market is shrinking. This means that reskilling the current workforce is a priority (OECD, 2019). At Unilever, they are taking a proactive stance to help workers develop a future-fit plan to learn new skills for a job that may not even exist at the moment.

BOX 3.3 RESKILLING FOR FUTURE FIT

Patrick Hull, Head of Learning and Future of Work, Unilever

The genesis of our Future of Work initiative was around 2018. The HR leadership team in Unilever was looking at the future of jobs report from the World Economic Forum. The report said that over the next five years, about 100 million jobs would change or go away and about 145 million would be new or substantially changed. The numbers really struck us. The report also said that the consumer goods industry would be one of the industries where the most significant change in jobs was likely to take place. Around 54% of roles were likely to change or be impacted. Assuming you have a manufacturing operation, as well as sales and back office, changes were anticipated through automation, robotics, AI, or other new ways of working. We were looking at half of our employee population or even more needing to reskill—not just to get better at their current jobs, but to anticipate changes in their field; for example, a finance professional needing to become a data specialist because that's the rising and emerging job.

How were we going to start doing that? At that stage all of our learning was about functional expertise—for example, getting finance people better at finance, marketing people better at marketing, salespeople better at sales. We were not thinking about how a salesperson could adopt radically different ways of selling, or where their skills could match with emerging roles in the organization. We therefore had to do the thinking: putting together a group of people to look into future-fit skills and to understand if consumer goods as an industry was going to be affected. What roles were going to be changing and in what ways? What were the likely impacts? And how could we start preparing our people for that? I was part of the group looking at this.

We had a very strong relationship then with the World Economic Forum and so leveraged their expertise and thinking to understand these issues better. In 2019 we ran an experiment across different parts of Unilever. We partnered with the World Economic Forum and SkyHive (https://www.skyhive.ai/)—a technology partner that collates and reviews labor market data, statistics, all the CVs that are out there, all the jobs that are on offer, in order to look at what are the declining jobs, what are the emerging jobs at a regional level. You can't just tell someone to reskill for a job that's going to be in Bangalore, India. They need to reskill for jobs in their locale. They also look at the different salary ranges jobs offer. If you are reskilling someone, you ideally want them to reskill into a job that's offering them better potential. They also look at the automation potential of those jobs.

We put forward a few Unilever roles into the mix and said, "Well, looking at these roles, what skills do they have? What is the automation potential of these roles and what could these roles realistically reskill into?" We did that for a cross-section of roles across our Unilever organization—in manufacturing, procurement, and in sales—in order to get a sense of likely changes for people here. SkyHive is predominantly North America-based, but they also have capability in Latin America and Europe, so we chose those three regions as initial spaces to look at the difference for the same role, but in different locations. We discovered that skills are a lot more applicable across roles than we thought. We found, for example, that some of our manufacturing roles could fairly easily reskill as solar panel technicians. It's a growing industry, a green industry, a very close match in terms of skills, and with readily available training for people to do that.

Whilst that's not within Unilever, it was good to know there's opportunities for our people outside. If automation in our factories leads to a lack of opportunities in Unilever, we could see a way forward to help them into other in-demand roles. Equally, we saw that, for example, our finance team's skills have got great applicability in the data science space, which is a big emerging area for our business. In fact, we are constantly struggling to find and keep people in those roles because of the competitive labor market and competition from companies like Google and Facebook. But we could offer an exciting opportunity to some of our finance professionals: "Hey, you could reskill to become a data scientist and have a really strong future career within Unilever." And it wouldn't take much effort to reskill people within that area.

We're now on a different path in terms of L&D. We're not here to just help finance professionals become better finance professionals. We will still do that. But we will also help people reskill to create opportunities, and we will show people how they can shift their career to different parts of the organization. We started doing this for people who were in roles which we anticipated might be impacted in the future.

So that brought us into thinking, how do we help people? Because there's training, but mainly it's more practical on-the-job experience people needed. This led to thinking about our flex model, where we allow people to spend 20% of their time working in different parts of the business on a different project. We've brought that to bear for this situation. Sales in this instance can give a project to a person from procurement, and it gives them a chance to get to know them and see their capabilities. Equally they get a chance to experience the sales organization without committing to it full time. Both parties get to suss one another out and also see the potential.

We found that was quite important because this concept is a bit difficult for the manager to grasp. People said: "I'm in the sales organization, I need someone with sales experience." We replied: "Oh no, we're bringing you someone from procurement." How would that work? We had to overcome that barrier. We saw this flex resourcing model as a way for people to learn, and also, a way to get that human dimension working. The relationship was going to be so key. That's been quite a powerful unlock for us. It's not a different way of learning, but we are more intentional about on-the-job learning while also helping people discover different departments and functions in the organization and experience them. They get some training support to learn the basics of the function while they're doing this. But they can also carry on in their current job for 80% of their time, while spending 20% on this; and then figure out if that is where they want to go with their career and what they want to reskill into.

Future Fit Planning

This has been a big shift in the way we're looking at learning and development at Unilever, bringing in formal reskilling rather than just upskilling, which is the standard way we've been doing learning and development. We now work with all employees. We're helping them all create their own Future Fit Plan. Do they want to upskill in their current functional area by following established L&D paths? Do they want to reskill—either inside Unilever or even start looking at reskilling outside? We're trying to be open and honest with people, advising them to also look at outside opportunities because potentially that's a better route and we'll support them with that option. We help them through that—starting with purpose, i.e., where do they see themselves in life? What impact do they want to make? We support them with wellbeing activities through this because it can be challenging to think about the reskilling option.

It starts with purpose. Since 2016, we've had around 50,000 Unilever employees, roughly a third of our organization, go through a purpose workshop. This is a workshop to help them understand their individual purpose. It's got nothing to do with linking your purpose to the organization. It's about understanding who you are as an individual and what you uniquely bring to your role in Unilever. People share their stories of crucible moments, i.e., moments they are most proud of, what they enjoyed doing as a kid, their superpower or a hobby, etc. We help them develop this red thread we call "purpose," which is what's unique about the way they approach situations and what they uniquely get energy from doing. For me, my purpose is to bring the essence of Pollyanna into the room. For me, it's all about bringing joy and innovation and a different way of seeing things. That's what gets me going. That's what's unique about me that I can bring to any job or role. It's how I uniquely approach that role.

People find phrases that are keys to unlock the way in which they need to turn up. It's role agnostic, but it can inform some of the roles they might want to take on. It also informs the learning and development needed to achieve that, the sorts of experiences to have, and makes sure managers are aware of what they uniquely bring to whatever roles they might be going into. We didn't want the starting point to be: "Reskill or you are going to lose your job to the robots." Starting people from fear and uncertainty isn't what we wanted. We wanted to start from, "Hey, you are in control of this. You decide where you want to be going in the future. It's based on your purpose and what you can uniquely bring and then use that purpose as your guide for roles and learning and development that you want to take on going forward." We've tried to reframe the future of work as a positive experience that they feel in control of, rather than what is being done to them. This was very intentional. If people are starting from a place of fear, their whole mind space is just going to narrow down. Their whole perspective is "let me protect myself," fight or flight versus open. Instead, we ask them to consider options and be prepared to try new things—a more expansive, open, positive framing.

If you were an employee, you would identify the top three skills you want to develop to become future fit. We have a matching tool. You enter your current skills, and much as does Amazon, using AI, the tool says that people like you have also said they've got these other skills. People often underrepresent their skills. If they identify ten skills, when we actually look at their job, we can interpolate maybe 30 additional skills for them. When you've got a bigger set of skills as your base, it then matches you against all the different job families that are available, and creates role plans. They're not specific jobs, but job areas or job families within Unilever. The AI says your skills match 80% with these other roles in the organization. So it opens people's eyes to possibilities outside their own function. For example, people in our factory environments actually also had a strong correlation with lab technician roles. We've got big R&D centers right next door to many of our factories, but we've never in the past helped people reskill into R&D from the factory environment.

Based on those matches, they have a chat with their manager and then have a conversation about whether they want to carry on in the current function and upskill in it, or instead consider reskilling and a move to something else. Then they choose their future-fit skills based on which path they want to take. We provide the learning and development support. They could do the flex experience; they can get mentors; they get all the support they need to carry on that journey, and also to look outside. At the moment, the matching tool only matches with jobs in Unilever, but external matching could be eventually considered.

We use Degreed as our learning experience platform and our people add the new skills they are developing to their Degreed profile. We call them "focus skills" and Degreed will push content based on those skill areas to them: either internal training we offer or other general courses sourced externally. We've also signed up to LinkedIn Learning and Udemy to provide additional sources of learning courses.

When our people have their six-month reviews with their manager, they do a skills review. They analyze what have they done to grow those skills, which could be going on a training program, completing a flex experience, or working with a mentor. They'll review their skill level and whether they need to do more. The manager could suggest other things to incorporate into their future journey. Our intention for the future is that once people reach desired skill levels, we can use our talent management system to promote job opportunities to them. In this way, we will help match people and their skills much better with the right opportunities.

Reskilling employees for jobs outside of the function they are in is not something that comes naturally to most managers. We are starting to address this, being clear that reskilling employees needs to be a core line manager capability. One of our standards of leadership is Talent Catalyst, which is about leaders inspiring and creating the right connections and opportunities for the people they manage. Managers need to be the catalyst for their people, helping them to identify skills and look at opportunities.

Employees also are only going to buy into this need to reskill if they can see rewards either in terms of better jobs or getting recognized. We're trying to integrate skills into every process, talent, recruitment, performance management, recognition, so that we create this red thread for people showing that investing in skills is going to help on their career journey.

Our job is to develop a renewable workforce and within that, bring in a new arm to L&D, which is reskilling. That's a big shift. An additional challenge is helping people approach this from a positive point of view, ensuring that clarity of purpose can help employees take ownership of this journey. And it helps us. It's a better way to engage with people in terms of their skill development and learning. What it means, then, is that L&D professionals need to do two things. One, we need to get better at reskilling people, taking someone with an existing skill set from an existing function into something different. And then, two, creating the optimal reskilling learning journeys for people that are not too onerous, don't require people to reinvent themselves completely, rather acquire the right skills in a practical, manageable way.

This unlocks new and different career options for our L&D team because they can work across different parts of the organization rather than always being tied to a particular academy or area of work. So they have new and better opportunities. It is also an increasingly integrated role with other parts of the organization and a blurring of boundaries—for example working hand-in-glove with other HR/People specialists such as reward, talent, organizational development (OD), learning grouping. I partner constantly with my colleagues to make this happen.

Another theme emerging in conversations we have had with L&D leaders is stronger partnerships between learning and organization development. Strategic learning requires an organization-wide perspective. Partnering brings strengths to both functions, a broader vision for learning and development, and access and support at the highest levels to implement initiatives.

CONCLUSION

This chapter has highlighted the role of digital transformation, skilling, and the future of work in rethinking L&D—trends that reappear in vignettes across chapters. The vignettes show how practitioners have leveraged technology demands to address the complexity intelligent technologies have created in work, learning, and in fostering networks and ecologies. The next two chapters show how technology opens new avenues for leveraging and understanding informal and incidental learning in complex circumstances.

4. Learning informally at work

INTRODUCTION

Knowledge-based work has introduced new forms of organization that, in turn, call for continuous learning—often just-in-time, micro-sized, and tailored to specific needs—aided by intelligent technologies. Intelligent technologies create new demands on human learning, often in partnership with machine learning.

These technologies have enabled learning and development (L&D) to recast informal and incidental learning from a "bit player" to central starring roles in organizational productivity. It is not that formal training has disappeared; it is differently designed and delivered, and decentralized to meet learner preferences. Organizations seek to pre-design, curate, and intentionally support and reward learning anywhere and anytime.

In this chapter, we examine ways L&D is rethinking informal learning in this shift, informal learning being somewhat conscious, if not explicitly intentional—in contrast to incidental learning (see next chapter). Knowledge workers, especially younger generations, expect jobs will provide for their continual growth. Many jobs that do not call for learning are being automated, but even in routine, less knowledge-rich work, there is an expectation that workers learn continuously. This demands rethinking, as well, of jobs, skills, and organizing for work.

DEFINING INFORMAL LEARNING

Informal and incidental learning (IIL) are interrelated, but they also play different roles and meet different needs. They work in tandem, and at times in partnership. Marsick and Watkins (1990) defined informal learning in contrast to formal training and education, even though they recognize that IIL can occur anywhere, any time, and in any place, including classrooms. IIL is "predominantly experiential and non-institutional" (p. 7). It is learner-initiated, not organization-initiated. Informal learning is conscious, though not highly structured, and is intentional. Incidental learning, by contrast, is "unintentional, a byproduct of another activity." It is "tacit, taken-for-granted, and often implicit in assumptions and actions" (p. 7).

Marsick and Watkins' IIL model (see Figure 4.1) shows how people informally and incidentally learn from experience. Learning starts with recognizing, examining, and diagnosing gaps in the situation, followed by an exploratory phase of looking for solutions; an implementation phase of choosing and enacting a solution; and an assessment phase of examining intended and unintended consequences. This process leads to confirming or adjusting one's understanding in preparation for future action. Elements of this cycle resemble the plan–do–check–act quality cycle. However, our model focuses on the need to learn when confronted with unknown aspects of a situation that are embedded in a context that needs unpacking due to the presence of multiple stakeholders and situational and organizational factors. The choice of a solution and its implementation may call for novel practices not yet encountered, mastered, or even imagined. Enactment might call for experimentation with new skills and tweaks added to recommended processes. The assessment might extend beyond feedback on accuracy to ripples and effects outside of the immediate context. Probing the context is often rich with exploration of less obvious, even implicit considerations, whereas explicit learning steps may involve habit, checklists, best practices, and lessons from prior experiences.

Development of our model was influenced by learning-from-experience theories of John Dewey (1938), Jack Mezirow (1978), Chris Argyris (1982), and Donald Schön (1984), among others (Marsick & Watkins, 1990). We situated IIL in non-routine decision making about action in the face of unknown circumstances. We turned to both Schön (1984) and Herb Simon's (1965) theorizing about decision making to understand learning involved with problem setting and solving in new contexts (Marsick & Watkins, 1990, p. 204). Learning is often prompted by, and tied to, steps taken in decision making.

We revisited this model in light of research. We added consideration of environmental factors based on Cseh's study of Romanian entrepreneurs as they transformed their businesses from a planned to a market-driven economy after the Cold War ended (Cseh et al., 1999). We added leadership and organizational lenses, drawing from our work on the learning organization. Ellinger and Cseh (2007) paid particular attention to the central unifying role of "learning-committed leadership" in navigating context. While learning at or through work could be individualized and self-directed, such learning is also frequently collaborative and social in nature. This is in line with Eraut's (2004) research on informal learning at work that demonstrates it is highly social, situated, and collaborative in nature.

Context changes all the time due to complexity. How, then, is L&D rethinking informal learning in light of this complexity? We see a growing shift toward curated and connected learning in the flow of work—a natural location for supporting informal learning. As L&D rethinks learning, technology puts

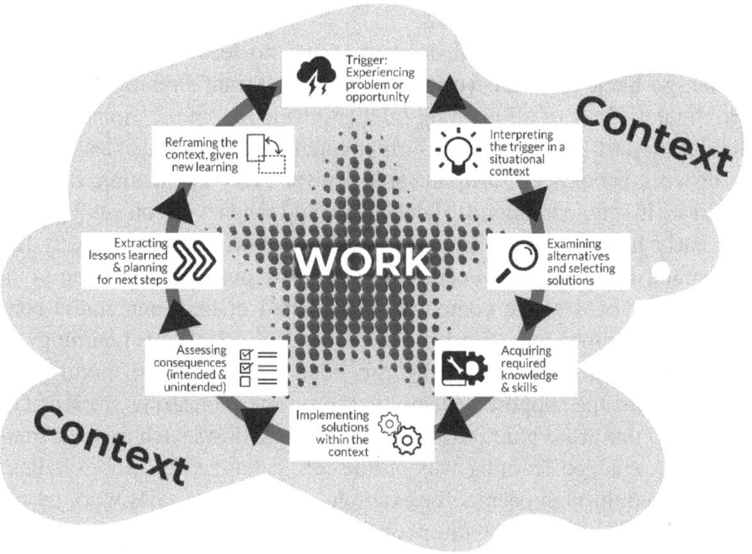

Source: Unpublished Graphic by Dimitri Papanagnous, M. D., Sidney Kimmel Medical College, Thomas Jefferson University. Adapted from Watkins KE, Marsick VJ, Wofford MG, Ellinger AD. The evolving Marsick and Watkins (1990) theory of informal and incidental learning. New Direct Adult Continuing Educ. 2018; 2018:21–36.

Figure 4.1 Marsick and Watkins' informal and incidental learning model

human and informational resources in the hands of anyone who has access to the internet. We share examples of how such learning can be scaffolded.

LEARNING IN THE FLOW OF WORK

Informal learning is a key component of learning in the flow of work—a modality that Josh Bersin (2018) believes is becoming dominant. Intelligent technologies make it possible to learn anywhere, anytime, and any place to meet immediate learning needs and preferences. Increasingly people learn just-in-time when they encounter on-the-job challenges. Learning management platforms—coupled with machine learning and artificial intelligence—have opened the door to learner experience offerings, providing a choice of learner-centric, self-directed paths to meet personalized needs. Mobile learning devices enable field workers to access videos, templates, or checklists as needed. Learners still consume macro-learning courses on their own time and at their own pace, but the trend is toward micro-learning at the moment of need.

As Bersin (2018) explained, learners want "to learn something, apply it, and then **go back to work**" (original bolding). Bersin's research "found that approximately 50% of all learning interactions is for 'in the moment of need' technical support" (p. 11). Bersin further concluded that, while "learning in the flow of work is not necessarily the solution for every application, it's coming fast and … it's the paradigm [to] design around whenever you can" (p. 13).

An early harbinger of learning-in-the-flow-of-work solutions was IBM's On-Demand Learning Architecture, which grew out of research on younger learner preferences at the company. It consisted of three integrated components: Work-Embedded, Work-Enabled, and Work-Apart Learning (IBM Learning Solutions, 2006). Work-Embedded Learning used modified electronic performance support systems (based on the pioneering work of Gloria Gery, 1991) that were built into identifiable work flows such as sales transactions. Work-enabled learning was on-the-job, catalyzed by work challenges, and supported through peers—for example, coaching on sales work by a peer who successfully partnered with specialized-focus clients. Work-apart learning was modularized training, streamlined and focused to meet particular needs.

Rethinking the Workplace Learning Paradigm

Learning in the flow of work ideally builds a learning-rich environment so that moving into learning mode is easy, accessible, expected, and rewarded. A high-impact learning organization survey (Bersin, 2017) conducted by Dani Johnson found that L&D functions "have moved beyond L&D and training; instead they are developing their entire organization to fully integrate learning within the flow of work and at the point of need" (p. 1). The research identified four stages of technology-driven learning maturity that move successively toward decentralized, personalized, self-driven, continuous, autonomous learning supported by peers, supervisors, and L&D. L&D is at first program and course driven, and then moves to learner-choice personalized approaches. As organizations mature, L&D shifts focus toward creating the right culture and environment for learners to drive their own learning. Using intelligent technologies, L&D further incorporates "feedback loops and data into the design of work so employees have consistent access to performance information that can help them improve within the current system while also contributing to decisions about how to modify or evolve that system" (Bersin, 2017, p. 3).

Bersin's (2017) research tracked impact on organizational results. Using "a three-year average for two financial performance metrics" (p. 3), researchers found that "maturity matters to an organization's bottom line." The trends Bersin identified have continued to evolve. In a 2019 Deloitte podcast hosted by David Mallon (2019, Capital H, Season 1, Episode 3) on learning in the flow of work, for example, Meriya Dyble described her L&D role as "connected learning" at ATB Financial. Reflecting George Siemens' (2004) "connectivism" theory that expects people to learn on their own in self-directed ways by building and drawing on extensive personal and machine networks, ATB Financial (online banking) "connect[s] people" to resources (information, experiences, people) rather than creating and delivering content to support growth. Connections are personalized. Their strategy is decentralized, democratized learning approaches. ATB applies their customer-centric approach to all employees: "We hire thousands of people a year and there is not one of those thousand people that should be onboarded in the same way as the other." Once on board, employees can access a learning platform that anticipates and curates experiences to meet employees' learning growth needs.

Scaffolding Learning in the Flow of Work

Not all employees are prepared to self-manage their learning, and not all managers are skilled in supporting them. Ray Jimenez developed a practice-based, technology-supported approach to rethinking how to engage and support employee learning. Jimenez focused on Bersin's guidelines: less focus on courses, more use of metrics to help learners guide their own learning, support for organic learning in the workflow, and expectation that learning will occur through trial and error, mistakes and experimentation (Hiipakka, 2018).

Jimenez (2019) developed a workflow diagnostic model that parallels steps in the Marsick and Watkins' IIL model, but with more emphasis on acting through work and less on balancing that with intentionally acquired skills for implementing new solutions to non-routine problems. His steps are: (1) diagnose/examine by looking at consequences and benefits; (2) fix, solve, and improve by seeking answers and solutions; (3) apply solutions through successive approximation and trial and error; and (4) see if answers and solutions work through feedback and metrics. Jimenez's design begins with "workers pay[ing] attention to their work" because that is frequently highly motivating. He assumes, "the fastest way to learn is to ask peers, leaders, suppliers and others for answers," which is the second step, though it does not preclude accessing other formal knowledge or resources. Finally, Jimenez "promotes big picture thinking." This "critical thinking" process "improves the quality and reliability of the answers, allows workers to avoid biases due to skills, roles and functional silos—created by organizational politics and cultural influences—to a better understanding of other business and operational goals" (p. 53).

In rethinking L&D in the workflow, Jimenez identified several challenges related to legacy learning systems. For example:

> Symptomatic of the cultural constraint was the question: "Who decides what is a correct answer?" … We wanted to show them that knowledge and solutions can also come from the workers, not just SMEs [Subject Matter Experts] and other experts. (Jimenez, 2019, p. 71)

Learning in the workflow is based on trial-and-error and successive approximation, which is "a natural part of work." However, support for experimentation requires change in norms, expectations, and "rewards." In some professions and businesses—for example, medicine, nuclear energy, firefighting, to name a few—mistakes can be a life-and-death matter. They may lead to loss of job or status or other psychological or mental stresses (Jimenez, 2019, p. 96). Learning today calls for changes in the organizational system as a whole, not only in the way people learn.

DIGITAL COACHING

Learning in the flow of work—whether 10-minute micro-learning or longer learner-directed modules on learner experience platforms—is a way of putting control for learning in the hands of intrinsically motivated, purpose-driven employees who continuously learn. Roshan Bharwaney works for a global social media company as a learning strategist in the operations department. His role is focused on enhancing the learning and performance of people who keep the company's platforms (apps) safe for community members and marketers. The major responsibility of the department is to block and remove harmful or violating content posted by users (i.e., community members and marketers) based on the policies developed with product teams, partners, governments, and regulators. Billions of people use the company's platforms daily, and content moderation work involves tens of thousands of human reviewers, including vendors, contractors, and employees, working in a 24/7, 365 days per year operation across the globe involving millions of transactions daily in over 100 languages.

BOX 4.1 SHIFTING FROM OFFSITE TRAINING TO LEARNING IN THE FLOW OF WORK

Roshan Bharwaney

The moment in time that signaled to me learning and development was evolving was when I started working in my new role. My role is situated in a technology company that places a high value on innovation. The company rewards employees who devise impactful innovations and implement them.

Many corporations take their learners out of production activities and have them participate in instructor-led, e-learning, or blended training programs. Taking people away from their work can reduce their overall productivity at training. The interrupted training process may not cover all the knowledge needed, and much of the training content may not be remembered at the time the worker needs to draw on that knowledge. The digital coach I am developing is embedded in work practices, and will enable my clients to partner with Artificial Intelligence (AI) to learn in the flow of work.

The Digital Coach

I support a large, global workforce of vendors, contractors, and employees who review social media content posted on company platforms that have been flagged by the company algorithm or by community members. The algorithm can review and take down the majority of violating content (e.g., most instances of nudity) though more complex and nuanced content requires human review (e.g., some types of hate speech). Flagged content is reviewed against policy, operational guidelines, special exception guidelines, and other company guidelines to decide whether to delete the content or leave it up. Content moderation policies are updated regularly and reviewers need to be aware of these latest changes. Reviewers spend a significant amount of time researching information to help them with decision making, particularly if they have a piece of content in front of them to review that is ambiguous and requires their critical thinking skills.

Due to COVID-19 restrictions, I have not yet met content moderators in person. Many tasks and processes that were always performed in offices are now done virtually. Since taking up my role, I have worked in virtual and hybrid environments. To learn how content moderators work, I attended a version of their onboarding training. I have also attended virtual job shadow sessions, where they perform their work and talk through how they look up information and make content decisions under review.

To help with their research and decision making, I am developing a digital coach tool to be embedded in the review tool. It will be used while working to look up and learn timely, relevant information to help reviewers with decision making (i.e., it helps provide just-in-time learning). The tool organizes policies, guidelines, and training information, including job aids and examples. This tool reduces the need for training on frequently updated policies, and thus cognitive load. The digital coach tool will increase accuracy and reduce average handling time per job. It should also shorten onboarding by reducing the search for required content.

We're developing and testing a prototype, and will collect data to help train the AI system to help make this a "smart" digital coach. The next generation of this tool will be supported by AI, which can better guide learners to the most appropriate sections of policies and training materials based on a scan of the content a reviewer is being asked to moderate.

Rethinking L&D through Building Innovative Prototypes

Working on the digital coach project, I felt the excitement of novelty and of stepping beyond the typical scope of Learning & Development professionals. Like many L&D professionals, in my career I focused on developing, managing, and facilitating learning programs, whether instructor-led, e-learning, or blended learning. The work on the digital coach looks at how people work and how to help them learn in the flow of their work. The work entails curating and orchestrating all the resources people need to enable their effective performance and this means I am driving worker performance, not just their learning. When an L&D professional focuses on performance, it helps them to shift to a more central role in the business. I also feel excited to be working with artificial intelligence, which will give the content moderation workforce the ability to focus on the more nuanced, unclear jobs, while the AI takes care of the simpler work.

I made decisions in consultation with colleagues with subject matter expertise (e.g., data science, user interface design, and project management). I focused on building a prototype digital coach, and testing it to optimize the design and functionality before implementing it more widely. The test-and-learn approach serves me well, because this is the first time I've worked on this type of tool and it's the first time a tool like this is being used by the company. To build a suitable digital coach, you need to put the right amount and type of information in front of the learner, without overwhelming them, and allow them to control the flow, quantity, and complexity of information they view.

Roshan's example focuses on improving a particular situation using digital coaching in relatively controlled contexts. This step is in the service of an ambiguous goal: removing harmful or violating content from social media in a dynamical context where conditions are always changing.

SCAFFOLDING, TARGETING, AND SCALING ONBOARDING

Learning in the flow of work for onboarding small numbers of diverse professionals with specialized backgrounds can be challenging and expensive to develop. But that is the challenge at D. E. Shaw, an international investment management firm known for developing complicated mathematical models and sophisticated computer programs to guide investment decisions. In the next vignette, Adam Neaman describes the way he has rethought the scalability and scaffolding of L&D when onboarding a range of diverse professionals joining the firm. D. E. Shaw has modularized assets so that, over time, L&D can scale onboarding initiatives in different functions to meet widely varied onboarding needs and time frames.

BOX 4.2 SCALABLE ONBOARDING SOLUTIONS FOR ROLE-DIVERSE POPULATIONS

Adam Neaman, Vice President, Learning & Development, The D. E. Shaw Group

Given the escalating diversity of roles in most organizations in recent decades, many organizations struggle with the need to onboard people into those roles. Company-wide onboarding, where people network and learn about the business, culture, etc., often requires relatively little tailoring to different audiences within the business, so it can be developed at scale, with only minor variations for things like region and hire seniority. In contrast, role-specific onboarding where people build the skills they need to get up to speed in their individual jobs requires much more tailored programming. Finding ways to deliver that economically is a major challenge. Described below is an approach we've developed at the D. E. Shaw Group to help effectively deliver tailored, skill-focused, role-specific onboarding to groups who might make as few as two or three hires per year into a given role.

Part of the strength of the solution is its simplicity, so, rather than start with a theoretical explanation, we'll start by looking at screenshots of a sample "Onboarding Roadmap" web page that would support an onboarding program for people joining the hypothetical Human Resources Analytics (HuRA) team, a small, but important supporting function in a fictional company. Both the responsibilities of the job and the culture of the HuRA team are complex, so onboarding is designed to be a two-year journey.

Example Onboarding Roadmap

What you see below is a sample web page that's been set up to help new hires and their managers navigate HuRA's onboarding process. The specific content shown is fictional and purely for illustrative purposes. The two-year journey has been broken into six time periods, each corresponding to a tab across the top. As you might expect, onboarding is more intensive at the start, so the first six months are more densely packed than the remaining 18. The tab for months 4–6 is shown in Exhibit Figure 4.2.1.

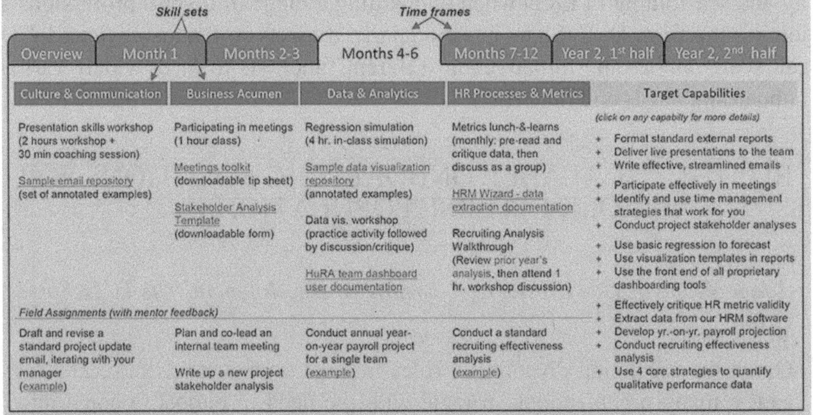

Source: Author.

Figure 4.2.1 Onboarding roadmap (hypothetical example)

In the right column under the tab is a list of **target capabilities**. The titles at the tops of the other columns are **skill sets**. Under each skill set is a list of **offerings** and **field assignments**. This sequencing roughly corresponds to the order in which Onboarding Roadmaps are developed, as displayed in Figure 4.2.2. Populating the roadmap with existing formal and informal learning supports tends to reveal gaps between target capabilities and available offerings, which can inform decisions about where to invest in more formal learning and/or add field assignments.

Development Step	Output	Why it's Useful
1. Define the **target capabilities**	A list of what people should be able to do by the end of a given time period	Helps align managers and new hires on performance expectations. The process of developing this list also helps align managers on business priorities
2. Break the target capabilities into **skill sets**	These are simply pithy names for gross categories (Business Acumen, Analytics, HR Knowledge, etc.)	Provides a shared conceptual and literal vocabulary to help managers and new hires plan, evaluate, and discuss development Limiting to 4–6 skill sets helps people organize their thoughts and have conversations along the lines of "You're really strong on Analytics and Business Acumen; I think you should focus your efforts on deepening your HR knowledge"
3. Identify **offerings** and **field assignments** to develop the skill sets	A list of available classes and resources, as well as field assignments, to help the new hire build each skill set	Maps learning needs to both formal and on-the-job learning activities and provides a guide that leads people through the onboarding process

Source: Author.

Figure 4.2.2 Process for developing onboarding roadmaps

Note, there's really a step 2.5, in which the target capabilities are divided into **time frames** (e.g., which Business Acumen skills should new hires aim to develop in months 2–3 vs. months 4–6).

A well-designed roadmap aligns new hires and their managers on performance expectations over a series of time horizons and shows them the activities and resources available to help them meet those expectations. It also provides them with a shared vocabulary for discussing, planning, and evaluating the new hire's development.

Developing many roadmaps is viable because they leverage existing infrastructure

In any *successful* organization, a sufficient amount of onboarding happens whether there is an onboarding program or not. It may not be as effective and efficient as it could be and it may not be delivered consistently, but much or most of what needs to be in place for new hires to build the skills they'll need is, in some form, being provided. In small teams, this typically includes things like:

- 1:1 sessions between experienced team members and the new hire

- sample documents (whether in a curated repository or simply shared ad hoc)
- process documentation and other reference materials
- various informal opportunities for apprenticeship and other on-the-job learning
- a small set of formal learning offerings, typically targeting a broader audience.

Our new approach to onboarding roadmaps takes advantage of these existing activities and resources. A two-year onboarding roadmap might list between 40 and 100 learning activities and resources. While that might sound daunting to develop, in the first roadmap we developed, roughly 90% of the activities and resources already existed in some form.

Once the target capabilities have been defined and divided up into time frames, a majority of the onboarding roadmap is created by simply mapping the existing offerings and opportunities for on-the-job practice (i.e., field assignments) across the time frames. This formalizes things that were previously informally in place.

The effort involved in doing the mapping is minimal and it immediately helps identify gaps where existing activities and resources may be insufficient to build the target capabilities. At that point you can have a conversation with the business about where it would be worth investing in developing more learning activities and resources to close the gaps.

Benefits of this approach

By putting formal structure around informal learning that is already in place, this solution provides an economically viable way to develop multiple small-audience onboarding programs tailored to a wide variety of different needs. Creating this structure not only increases the consistency of onboarding experiences, it also provides a vocabulary and conceptual framework for new hires and their managers to plan and manage development.

The modular assets approach at D. E. Shaw provides an adjustable framework to rethink tailored onboarding for diverse hires in order to guide just-in-time learning. New hires follow a learning path that takes their prior knowledge and skill into consideration. The roadmap guides the performance conversations managers have with them. Tangible supports, mapped to specific capabilities, can be anticipated. Additionally, the business can use the process to periodically reflect on its development needs, set priorities, and assess whether further supports are needed to reach capability targets.

INFORMAL LEARNING WHEN CHALLENGES LEAN TO THE COMPLICATED OR COMPLEX

The examples provided thus far do not enter the territory of extreme complexity. Complexity calls for adaptive learning and leadership (Heifetz et al., 2009) when clear answers and technical solutions are not adequate for the situations being faced. The Cynefin framework (Snowden & Boone, 2007) is a heuristic for diagnosing when circumstances are simple, complicated, complex, or chaotic. Decisions are simple (and often evidence-based) when outcomes from actions are predictable. They are complicated when solutions can be found but they call for specialized knowledge and experience. They are complex when the situation is completely unpredictable and ever changing, calling for exploratory actions to create alternatives, or where the situation is outright chaotic or totally unmanageable.

Learning in the workflow is easier to design when solutions are clear and predictable. As circumstances become complicated, learners need more creative ways to reach desired outcomes. Accessing this knowledge often calls for conversation with peers who have successfully navigated such challenges. But how can one find and get access to this help?

One approach to doing so is directed performance support (DPS) (Neaman & Marsick, 2018). Neaman designed DPS for current work challenges that are not clearly structured, but are highly motivating—and for which some resources can be identified to help explore solutions. For example, if a learner is preparing an opening conversation with a client, the learning designer might construct a conversation planner that includes resources to stretch their thinking. Resources are for the learner's discretionary use. The task is "to come up with answers that leave you prepared for a compelling, insightful conversation with your client" (Neaman & Marsick, 2018, p. 8). Collaboration is designed into the learning and typically freely offered based on peers' experience with similar circumstances. Learners are invited to "share work with peers and seek their input. They do get feedback, but much of it is also performance support in the form of insight sharing and problem solving" (p. 8).

Knowledge workers may seek to move aspects of complex decisions to the complicated domain in order to probe the limits of what is known as a step toward sensing and responding to complex circumstances. A good example of this comes from a study we are engaged in related to how physicians made decisions in the emergency room and intensive care unit in the early stages of the COVID-19 pandemic (Papanagnou et al., 2022). Physicians practice evidence-based medicine, so in the absence of evidence with this new disease, they looked at aspects of the disease they could treat using evidence-based medicine. In essence, they identified what they could safely do by consulting colleagues and searching for credible expert knowledge. They drew, for example, on experiences with lung disease in recent pandemics, such as HIV–AIDS and SARS. They pored through available information in China, Italy, and New York; consulted frequently with colleagues; and kept up to date with rapidly changing guidelines, rather than relying primarily on their own situational judgment acquired through prior experience. In essence, they restructured the situation to make it less complex so that it would be amenable to known interventions.

LEARNING-BASED COMPLEX WORK

This chapter's final example illustrates the way in which organically arising IIL is paired with opportunities to build knowledge through a combination of structured education and informal learning by peers working in frequently complex circumstances. Reda Sadki of The Geneva Learning Foundation (TGLF) rethought L&D for immunization workers in many roles in low- and middle-income countries (LMICs). Adapting to technology available to participants from the countries that joined this effort, Sadki designed a mix of experiences that broke out of the limits of "training" as it was often designed. He addressed,

> the inability to scale up to reach large audiences; difficulty to transfer what is learned; inability to accommodate different learners' starting places; the need to teach learners to solve complex problems; and the inability to develop sufficient expertise in a timely way. (Marsick et al., 2021, p. 15)

TGLF invited learners to create and share new learning to the social and behavioral challenges faced by frontline staff from all levels of immunization systems in low- and middle-income countries (LMICs). Sadki designed L&D for "in-depth engagement on priority topics," insights into "the raw, unfiltered perspectives of frontline staff," and peer dialogue that "gives a voice to frontline workers" (The Geneva Learning Foundation, 2022). Reda started with an e-learning course, which he supplemented by interactive, community building, and knowledge creation features offered by Scholar, a learning platform developed by Bill Cope and Mary Kalantzis (Marsick et al., 2021, pp. 185–186). Scholar's data analytics enabled him to tailor learning to learner preferences and to continually check outcomes and adjust next steps.

See Figure 4.3, which lays out the full learning cycle Reda implemented to support peer learning-based work—"work that privileges learning in order to build individual and organizational capacity to better address emergent challenges or opportunities" (Marsick et al., 2021, p. 177).

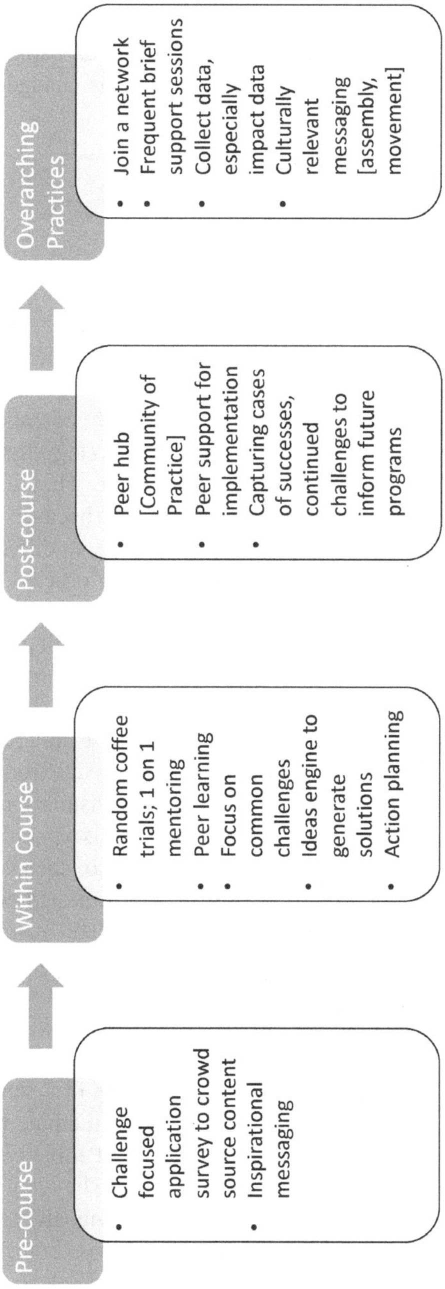

Source: Author.

Figure 4.3 *The TGLF full learning cycle*

In his initiative, over a period of 12–18 months, participants develop and implement projects related to local immunization initiatives. To date, participants have come from 120 countries. In this vignette, Reda Sadki reflects on how the approach evolved over time, and how L&D has changed in a connected, networked learning environment.

BOX 4.3 REFRAMING LEARNING AND DEVELOPMENT

Reda Sadki, President, The Geneva Learning Foundation

My reframe of L&D started when I wrote to Bill Cope and Mary Kalantzis, Directors of Common Ground Research Networks, when I was appointed Senior Officer for Learning Systems at the International Federation of Red Cross and Red Crescent Societies (IFRC), about my strategy for the organization of facilitation, learning, and sharing knowledge. They replied that these were interesting ideas, but I was missing the point because this is not learning! What I shared focused on *publishing* knowledge in different ways, but not on *creation of knowledge* as key to the learning process. That was a shock to me. So, the first realization about the limits of current thinking about L&D came from Bill and Mary challenging me by saying: "What are people actually getting to do? You know, that's where the learning is likely to happen."

I could see they had a point, but I didn't know what it meant. I reflected on recent work I had done for the IFRC, where I was responsible for a pipeline of 80 or so e-learning modules. These information transmission modules were extremely limited, had very little impact. But there is a paradox, which is that people across the Red Cross who we were trying to reach were really excited and enthusiastic about them. The learning platform had become the fastest-growing digital system in the entire Red Cross Red Crescent movement. I had not designed these modules. It was 500 screens of information with quizzes at the end. It violated every principle of learning design. And yet people loved it and were really proud to have completed it.

The second realization was that what made people excited using the most boring format and medium was that this was the first time in their life that they were connecting in a digital space with something that spoke to their IFRC experience. So, the driver was learning! People come to the Red Cross because they want to learn first aid skills. They want to learn how to prepare for a disaster or recover from one. Previously, that was an entirely brick-and-mortar experience. You have Red Cross branches pretty much everywhere in the world. It's a very powerful social peer learning experience. The trainer teaching you first aid is likely to be someone like you from your community. You meet people with like-minded values. It's a really powerful model. And so, however inadequate, the digital parallel to that existed, and it helped people connect with their Red Cross culture, but in the digital space.

The third insight was reading what George Siemens was writing in 2006. That was the connection to complexity in networks. I read Marsick and Watkins in the '80s and '90s, and then Siemens in the 2000s, on digital networks. The Internet leads to a different kind of thinking, and his theory of learning, connectivism, grew out of that difference. January of 2011, Ivy League universities began to publish massive open online courses (MOOCs). Stanford professors had 150,000 people in their artificial intelligence MOOC, versus 400 people who take the same course on the Stanford campus.

Sasha Poquet wrote a paper based on a social networking analysis of what we did during the COVID-19 Scholar Peer Hub. The COVID-19 Scholar Peer Hub was a digital network hosted by The Geneva Learning Foundation (TGLF). The Peer Hub launched in July 2020 and connected over 6,000 health professionals from 86 countries to contribute to strengthening skills and supporting implementation of country COVID-19 plans of action.

Sasha wrote about the value of a learning environment that builds a community of learning professionals, and that has ongoing activities to maintain the community both short- and long term, where you educate through various initiatives rather than create individual communities for each independent offering. That's where we have moved in rethinking Learning & Development. You help people learn by connecting to each other, and by understanding the informal, incidental nature of learning.

A colleague commented that in today's world, you're better off talking about digital networks than you are about communities of practice. Yet these are two competing frameworks that collide, contradict, and are superimposed on top of each other. Both are helpful at specific times. In general, you can recognize the tensions and say: "Well, let's put each one in front of the problem. Let's see what we gain by applying each. Let's reconcile in situ what the contradictory things are that we learn through these different lenses and then make decisions and figure out what the design elements look like."

What does it give to hold these notions of community and network in creative tension with one another? It depends on the context. It's kind of like a fruit salad where you mix all these fruits together and the juice you get at the bottom of the bowl tends to be really delicious! That's the best case. The flip side is confusion. Some categories of learners just feel completely overwhelmed by being presented with multiple ways of doing something, having to make their own decisions in ways they're simply not used to, being given too many choices or being put in contexts that are too ambiguous for there to be an easy resolution. But if you think about the skills we need in a digital age—for navigating the unknown, accepting uncertainty, making decisions, that ability to look around the corner—we try to convey the message to people who are uncomfortable that if they don't figure out how to overcome their discomfort, they're probably going to struggle and not be ready to function in the age in which we live.

Evolution of the Model

[Looking back to early 2020, Reda described the roots of this approach in an early pre-course symposium centered on video archives drawn from prior conferences sponsored by the Bill & Melinda Gates Foundation. Reda packaged selected talks in a daily sequence, and interspersed it with networking discussions and sharing of experiences of immunization training by field-based practitioners. Reda elaborated as follows.]

For many, it was the first time they could go online and read the experience of a peer. It was a process of discovery—realizing you can literally and figuratively connect across distance with people who are like yourself through Skype. We were able to create a conference-like experience, a metaphor that's familiar to many—the combination of presentation and conversation and shared experience—by basically Scotch-taping together some older videos and editing a few stories from the real world. Now, it was part of an overall process over several years that got us to that point—where we had formed a community, a digital community that was mature enough, that was sophisticated enough, to overcome the barriers they were facing and participate. But still, it showed it could be done!

We began to try out our new ideas. In a Teach to Reach Conference we designed, we set up opportunities for people to pair off and talk to one another about their field experiences with vaccination. We had some 56 workshops and formal sessions, but more participation was through some 14,000 networking meetings where you pressed a button and you were randomly matched with someone else at the conference. That gave birth to a quarterly event dedicated entirely to networking, which has continued to grow. People now choose a session where you discuss, you hear people sharing their insights and experiences of vaccine hesitancy, and then you go off and network and share your reflections on what happened in that group session; and also continue your learning in that very intimate way that you get in a sort of one-to-one conversation that you don't get in the anonymization of the Zoom rectangles.

The next step was the addition of a project around a real problem that participants face, and use of learning resources to support work on that project. An evaluation showed that people were already implementing projects and doing things with what they had learned. The course includes the development of an action plan, but in order to catalyze action on project plans, we added the Ideas Engine, where people share ideas and practices, and give and receive feedback on them. That's followed by situation analysis—really getting to the root cause of the problem they're facing (5 Whys supported by Total Quality Management). And third, then, is action planning to clarify: What's your goal? What are the three actions you're going to take? Do you have smart goals? It has taken years to unpack the pieces that encourage reflective practice, that will develop analytical competencies, higher order learning.

And that's followed by the Impact Accelerator—that doesn't have an end point. It's four weeks of goal setting. People initially set broad goals like, "By the end of the month I will have improved immunization coverage." We help them set specific goals: e.g., "By the end of the month, I will have presented the project to my boss and secured some funding"— and even that may be very ambitious! We help people figure out what they can actually do within the constraints they have. You don't have a competitive element, you don't have a financial incentive, and it still works. The heart and soul of it is intrinsic motivation.

After these steps there's ongoing longitudinal reporting. Basically, we'll call you back and ask, what happened to that project you were doing? Did you finish it? Did you get stuck? If so, why? What evidence do you have that it's made a difference? You share that with us and if you have good news to share, we'll probably invite you to an inspirational event for the next cycle.

Supports and Challenges

If you look at this from the point of view of the learner, the first point of contact is social. It's somebody they know who's going to share with them on WhatsApp the invitation to join the program. Second are steps that test motivation and commitment because they could be seen as barriers to entry, for example, a long questionnaire for the current full learning cycle. Close to 7,000 people have completed that. About 40% of people who start the questionnaire finish it, and then start receiving many emails to prepare for the next steps. We start with didactic steps, combined with some inspirational messages, e.g., asking them to reflect on why they are committed to the program, or how they are going to organize their time. We don't know what the program design will look like until we've collected the applications and analyzed what people share about their biggest challenges because it's all challenge-based. We think it's vaccine hesitancy, and vaccine hesitancy is right up there, but there may be some things that surprise us. And so, we adapt every part of the design, and we keep doing that every day throughout the program, so there's no disconnect between the design and the implementation.

In the course, the first thing is an inspirational event to connect with their intrinsic motivation, which we mobilize throughout the cycle. Yesterday, for example, we had an event for the network that completed the first part of the full learning cycle. We challenged people to share photos, showing them in the field, doing their daily work during World Immunization Week. We got over 1,000 photos in about a week. A big part of the event was just sharing the photos with music and reading the names of the people and their comments. A big chunk of it is in the affective domain of learning—that is really important and usually incredibly hard to get to. And what we saw were people in the room having those moments of coming to consciousness, realizing their problems are shared, and feeling stronger because of it.

People love peer learning in principle but still are wary. They might wonder how they can trust what their peer says: What's the proof I can rely on them? What happens if they let me down? How do I feel if I don't own up to the expectations? What if I'm peer-reviewing the work of somebody who's far more experienced than I am, or conversely, if I read somebody's work and judge they didn't have the time or make the effort to do something good?

If your project is due by Friday, there will be no extension, but by contrast, the choice of project is yours. We're not going to tell you from Geneva, Switzerland, what your challenge is in your remote village, so you define it. We'll challenge you to put yourself to the test, to demonstrate that this is actually your toughest challenge. Or to demonstrate that what you think is the cause is the actual root cause. And then we'll have a support system that has about 20 different ways in which people can not only receive support, but also give it to others. For the technical support session, we'll say there are two reasons for joining. Either you have a technical issue you want to solve; or you're doing so well, you have a little bit of time to give to help your colleagues.

It took us years to gain confidence in peer learning after we adopted it, and so we had a particularly challenging course. We had prior experiences with learners who wanted an expert to tell them if their assignment was good or not. Getting people to trust peer learning forced us to think through how we articulate the value of peer learning. How do we help people understand that the limitations are there, but that they do not limit the learning?

An assumption in global health is that, in order to teach, you need technical expertise. We consider subject matter expertise, but if you are an expert and come to our event, you're actually asked to listen. There's no presentation. You listen to what people are sharing about their experiences, and then you have a really important role, that is, to respond to what you've heard and demonstrate that your expertise is relevant and helpful to people who are facing these challenges. That has sometimes led to opposition when people understand to what extent we flipped the prevailing model around. Some people really embrace it. Others get really scared.

One of the shifts we have made is that we stopped talking about courses. It's a very useful metaphor, but here we're talking about the movement for immunization agenda 2030. In the past, we observed that people who dropped out felt shame and stopped participating. Even if you are not actively participating, you're still a member of the immunization movement! People have participated as health professionals, as government workers, as members of civil society, in various kinds of movements since decolonization.

We used to call the Monday weekly meeting a discussion group. We're now calling it a weekly assembly, drawing on language used by a Nigerian top global expert on immunization who understands both the community and the global dimension of healthcare. About ten years ago, I began to think of my goal for these discussion groups like the musician, the artist that you most appreciate, who really moves your soul, moves you, your every fiber and your body and your soul and your mind. I remember in 1989 I went to a Pink Floyd concert. When we left the concert, we were drenched in sweat; we were exhausted and just had an exhilarating experience. That's what I would like people who participate in our events to feel. I believe that's key to fostering the dynamics that will lead to effective teaching and learning and change as an outcome. We're still light years away from that.

CONCLUDING THOUGHTS

Informal learning is central to workplace learning today. The Marsick and Watkins model emphasizes organically arising, person-driven learning based on intrinsic motivation and environmental demand for continuous learning. The umbrella under which we discuss it here—learning in the workflow—is a framework in which the organization plays a key initiating role. Our model was created in the early days of knowledge work. Complexity today plays an even more central role in driving the way L&D is being rethought. At the same time, all situations calling for learning are not necessarily complex.

In today's continuous learning environment, L&D puts greater responsibility for learning in the learner's hands. Organizations partner with learners to create and provide resources for just-in-time learning. L&D has blurred lines across formal and informal learning to support continuous learning. Organizations do train for core competencies and some standardized solutions; but they also tailor and scaffold and personalize learning through practices and resources in the flow of work. At the same time, employees are helped to innovate and use their judgment to address learning needs that emerge in the moment. Learners become productive co-creators and co-producers of what is increasingly learning-based work (Marsick et al., 2021).

In the following chapters, we look at incidental learning and the learning organization, which build on the foundations seen here. Complexity has given rise to a more holistic and emergent approach to learning and development. Incidental learning emerges out of tasks, contexts, and situations. The culture that supports learning—especially informal and incidental learning—is one that is itself open and adaptive. These foundational theories guide our rethinking of L&D.

5. Learning incidentally in complexity—with Jill Karen Jinks

Marsick and Watkins (1990) define incidental learning as a subcategory of informal learning and as learning derived from a process that "takes place on a continuum of conscious awareness" (p. 13). Moreover,

> Incidental learning includes learning from mistakes (including how people frame experiences as mistakes), learning by doing (including trial-and-error experimentation), and learning through a series of covert interpersonal experiments .... The degree of conscious awareness of one's learning plays an important role in the clarity of learning .... Many times [incidental] learnings are unintentional consequences. (pp. 13–14)

It is our contention that incidental learning in these complex times is an increasingly significant mode of learning that can be facilitated by learning and development.

THE NATURE OF INCIDENTAL LEARNING

"We can know more than we can tell" is how Michael Polanyi (1966, p. 4) described tacit knowledge of humans. David Autor (2014) labeled this description as the Polanyi Paradox to highlight a basic element of incidental learning that cannot be emulated by machines—the innate ability of humans to acquire (through incidental learning) and deploy (as tacit knowledge) learning in

> tasks requiring flexibility, judgment and common sense [that] contemporary computer science seeks to overcome ... by building machines that learn from human examples, thus inferring the rules that we [humans] tacitly apply but do not explicitly understand. (p. 2)

This human ability to learn incidentally while self-organizing in novel situations is highlighted by Marsick and Watkins (1990). The authors conceptualized incidental learning as "a by-product of some other activity, such as task accomplishment, interpersonal interaction .... or trial-and-error experimentation. Incidental learning is never planned or intentional, whereas informal learning can be planned or intentional (p. 6). They add, "Incidental learning

… almost always takes place in everyday experience although people are not always conscious of it" (p. 12).

Consistent with Autor's (2014) description of the Polanyi Paradox, Marsick and Watkins emphasize meaning's playing a "central role in [human] learning" even though it is "difficult, if not impossible, to observe and measure behaviorally. Meaning is derived through reflection on experience" (1990, p. 20). Logically, a new construction can be observed as a change in behavior only after the meaning is made.

Marsick and Watkins believe, "informal and incidental learning are needed most when individuals experience a situation as non-routine. Learned responses and habitual ways of acting are least likely to work under novel conditions. The situation might be completely new and thus fully non-routine; or it might be potentially routine but treated as non-routine for some reason" (1990, p. 21). They also note the roughness and wholeness of the informal learning process, citing McClellan's (1983) descriptions of "the nature of the inquiry [in a non-routine situation as] 'messy, multivariate, back-forth-many-stages-all-at-once'" (p. 23).

Recognizing the nature of complex situations, Marsick and Watkins (1990) suggest incidental learning may be the more flexible and primary source of knowledge in responding to

> [a] given complex situation, when our attention is being pulled to a specific task, [and] we must decide what to include or exclude from our interpretation of a situation. We draw on our past experience and, most importantly, we typically draw on frameworks for understanding which we have already developed because we do not have time to build a new framework from scratch. It is only when we think that the framework does not match the experience that we develop a new framework. (p. 24)

Marsick and Watkins (1990) recognize, "the way in which a person frames or sets the problem [is a critical factor that delimits incidental learning], since the messy nature of reality does not easily lend itself to the scientific purity of laboratory conditions" (p. 25).

Responding to the novel and dynamic nature of edge-of-chaos states and situations may require individuals to "know more [and do more] than they can tell" by relying on the powerful domain of incidental learning (Polanyi, 1966, p. 4).

Weaving Complexity Science with Incidental Learning

Marsick et al. (2017) considered "where informal learning is situated in the continuum of ambiguity and unpredictability of complex learning situations, and how this understanding might reshape our perspective of informal learning" (p. 30). Complexity science offers a foundation for positioning human learning as part of the adaptive processes of dynamical systems.

> Complexity science helps us discern the characteristics of a context with regard to cause and effect—and if we pay attention—how to develop capacities to respond in ways that are closer to the reality of the context, situation, and/or event. (p. 30)

Recognizing the natural turbulence associated with most contexts, Marsick et al. (2017) accept Juarrero's (1999) description of complex systems as a "dynamic, a mess of interactions and relationships that are constantly evolving, creating ripeness for emergence, and a disruption of learned responses" (p. 30). Table 5.1 compares the original model with the proposed complexity inspired model.

Mitchell (2009) notes the adaptive behavior of complex systems is founded in their ability to self-organize through learning or evolutionary processes when faced with an environmental perturbation. Thus, we look at studies of learning in the midst of complex, ambiguous, edge-of-chaos contexts.

EMPIRICAL STUDIES OF INCIDENTAL LEARNING IN COMPLEX CONTEXTS

Jill Jinks (2022) reviewed empirical studies of human learning: in "organized chaos" contexts; associated with human innovation; identifying contextual influences on learning; discussing learning from failure, or from complexity. In each study, Jinks examined forms of informal and/or incidental learning as defined by Marsick and Watkins (1990) and as applied in complex environments.

The purpose of the Goldman et al. (2009) study was to "understand how, when, and why emergency medicine residents learn while working in the chaotic environment of a hospital emergency room" (p. 555). Using a qualitative interview methodology with thematic data analysis, four different types of learning episodes were revealed that

> varied in intensity, duration and the degree of motivation and self-direction required by the learner. One episode could prompt another. Learning occurred both individually and in social interaction in the workplace during the episode, as well as outside of the workplace environment after the experience had occurred. (p. 555)

Table 5.1 How complexity drives rethinking incidental learning

Select Dimensions of Marsick and Watkins Informal and Incidental Learning Model	Original: Model 1	Complexity: Model 2
What is informal and/or incidental learning in the workplace?	A challenge triggers a fresh look at the situation, followed by a search for alternative responses, taking action, and evaluating results; incidental learning is what occurs at the interstices, what emerges when we unintentionally learn something new	A process of discerning cause and effect in the obvious and complicated domains—informal learning produces good and best practice results in response to a recognized problem
Perceived relationship between forms of learning (formal, informal, and incidental)	Formal, informal, and incidental are a conceptual continuum of control over the learning process, on intentionality over what is learned	Informal learning is decoupled from incidental learning to enable a goodness-of-fit perspective of prevailing learning modalities in four domains. Informal fits with obvious and complicated domains; incidental fits with complex and chaotic domains
Who learns?	Individual	The system learns—the past is integrated with the present as the elements evolve with one another and with the environment
How learning occurs (processes and practices)	Contextually supported, often self-directed process of problem solving; incidental learning is a by-product of another activity that could be formal or informal learning (the hidden curriculum)	Relationships within the system are infused by contextual characteristics, history, and dynamic interactions, such that understanding, and perception emerge to generate action
Role of social interaction and social relations in learning	Unexplained	Complex systems are dynamic, a mesh of interactions and relationships that are constantly evolving creating ripeness for emergence and a disruption of learned responses

Source: Excerpted and adapted from Marsick et al., 2017, p. 31.

In the emergency room environment, these learners (residents) confront edge-of-chaos interactions repeatedly and must learn to create adaptive responses. The authors note:

> historically, environmental dynamics such as disruption, confusion and chaos were seen as negative factors, often indicating the impending demise of [a system]. Now these conditions are considered … to be normal and necessary …. Yet little is known about how people learn in a chaotic workplace environment. (p. 556)

The Goldman et al. (2009) study found four different types of learning activities or events: participation in the environment; focused learning moments; repetitive cycles; and intense experiences. The study concluded:

> learning in a chaotic environment does not involve substantially different learning facilitators than learning in a non-chaotic [environment]: observation, practice, mistakes, feedback, questioning, and reflection .... What is different about how learning occurs is the relationship of the episodes and the amount of motivation and self-direction required by the learner. (p. 568)

Taber et al. (2008) conducted a similar study examining how firefighters and paramedics learn in "grey" areas and organized chaos. Using a case study method in Canada, researchers studied about 900 paramedics and a firefighting department with approximately 400 firefighters. Data were collected by "in-depth, semi-structured interviews with senior administrators, training staff, and front-line personnel; observations of training sessions; and 'ride-alongs' with paramedics and firefighters in the field" (p. 277).

Consistent with the Goldman study, the researchers found "the notion of situated learning is insufficient to explain the dramatic performance of emergent, creative, and autonomous actions often required of individual emergency personnel in crisis situations" (Taber et al., 2008, p. 272).

In the case of the paramedics, "many held that, while the extensive protocols regulating work often provide a useful overarching frame for action, these protocols were inadequate for dealing with the 'grey areas'—situations unanticipated by the protocols" (p. 278). Specifically, the researchers concluded, "situated learning offers little help explaining the dramatic performance of emergent, creative, and autonomous actions often required of individual emergency personnel in crisis situations" (p. 273). The paramedics noted they

> do not necessarily follow the protocols exactly but make your own judgements .... You can adapt the protocol to fit ... and that's something you learn with experience ... not every case is going to be the same, because you have to adapt your treatment .... You are constantly adapting your pathway, choosing your protocol. (Taber et al., 2008, p. 279)

Firefighters emphasized complexity's influence:

> regardless of their level of training or previous experiences, they do not see any call as routine—anything can happen. Looking ahead, preparing for the worst, and being ready to adapt are keys to success in firefighting due to its unpredictable nature. (p. 280)

Firefighters willfully developed a process to organize chaos and coordinate action, helping all firefighters work as a team with one goal and assigned tasks. The researchers learned that the process as implemented

> more closely resembles a living organism than a static policy. Every call is unique and the responses to each call change depending on the situation and the personnel involved. It is this human element that takes a linear model and makes it adaptive because "everything is great on paper, but nothing ever goes that smooth" in reality. [We] must "organize chaos" and "adapt, adjust, adjust, adjust, adjust, adjust." (p. 281)

Much like the paramedics, the firefighters acknowledged the influence and impact of tacit (incidental) learning in operating in edge-of-chaos situations:

> One [firefighter] stated that what they do is impossible to describe and must be experienced personally to be understood. It is therefore very difficult to pass on these tacit understandings to new firefighters in any way other than engaging with them in the flow of unfolding situations. (p. 282)

The researchers acknowledged the incidental nature of this type of learning and how it influences

> the ability to respond to emergent situations, adapt policy into practice, and navigate through the grey areas and organized chaos of their professions. However, in these terrible moments, when all things anticipated or thought known dissolve, and when a firefighter or paramedic stands alone or with a comrade needing to make just the right decision, *another kind of active, creative, fast-as-lightening learning must be deployed.* (Taber et al., 2008, p. 284, italics added).

This tacit learning and knowledge may well be the organic, free-radical learning that is most prevalent in edge-of-chaos adaptive practices.

Research using context that is inherently an edge-of-chaos environment (emergency rooms, paramedics, and firefighting) confirms the self-organizing criticality that triggers an adaptive response through learning. The turbulent state of the context is obvious. The learners knowingly intervene and are comfortable with their ability to adapt to the unpredictability of interactions in the environment. The adaptive capacity and rate of adaptiveness are developed and sized for the controlled chaos. Further, reliance on tacit knowledge to provide additional adaptive capacity and to increase the rate of adaptiveness is suggested in these studies.

Findings from Harner (2013) are consistent with the other studies examined here. Harner studied incidental learning in a healthcare organization. Harner's (2013) research emphasizes incidental learning described by Marsick and Watkins (1990) as "[taking] place as a result of interactions with others without conscious intention of learning or knowledge acquisition" (p. 22). It is not goal oriented, but often the result of reflection. Harner (2013) quotes Reischmann (1986) in describing incidental learning as "learning en passant" to describe "learning taking place in life situations where there is nothing like prepared curriculum, learning is identified by looking back, and takes place when learning is not a prime motivation" (pp. 21–22).

Harner (2013) notes it is difficult, if not impossible, to isolate incidental learning from other kinds of learning in general, given that "[u]nanticipated ways of doing daily activities will emerge as a result of incidental learning" (p. 29). Incidental learning is best described as a context-inspired process that is engaged in rather than a predicted outcome.

Viewing incidental learning through the lens of complexity science, Harner (2013) notes the learning is governed by the interactions of the adaptive processes in a given context. The research environment is a patient-visit environment, which he describes as a complex adaptive system. Harner (2013) identifies a "hidden learning process" that arises out of inherent gaps in the formal and informal training processes. No matter how good the planning for systems, processes, or learning, gaps arise due to unknown or unpredictable factors:

> Insufficiencies in knowledge will force incidental learning to occur as employees look for solutions to unanticipated problems. Rapid decisions and instant responses required by time constraints result in incidental learning and subsequent unintended behavior that may or may not be desirable. (p. 43, italics added)

Harner discovered

> how incidental learning was embedded in the situation that each participant was describing. ... [This discovery] is consistent with its definition .... The situation [context] contributes to the incidental learning that many of the participants experience as they do their best to accomplish job tasks. (2013, p. 64)

The power of context to shape learning and development is particularly significant in incidental learning.

Silva (2007) used a hermeneutical phenomenological approach to gain insights into incidental learning with emphasis on the role of context, both situationally and from the "general perceptions and experiences of learning" described by participants (p. 5). The study included analysis of the occupational culture within which the participant engaged. Its central purpose was "an exploration of how individuals know they know when they learn something in the incidental manner." The researcher sought to "provide insights into why some individuals learn in a given situation while others do not" (p. 6).

Silva (2007) found that when the organizational context is aligned with the learner's preferred style of learning, incidental learning is greater. An individual's perception of learning "guides their openness to learning in certain situations" (p. 209). "Those [individuals] who tended toward a deep approach to learning had more incidental learning experiences to share and richer stories" (p. 210). Additionally, "most incidental learning in the workplace is validated in a manner akin to Schön's notion of reflection-on-action. In addition, in some instances participants checked with multiple sources or with 'experts'—those who should know about the topic at hand" (p. 213).

Innovation is a form of adaptation that relies on learning processes in humans (Holland, 1998). According to Cheng and Van de Ven (1996),

> the two most commonly-used explanations of the innovation process, that it follows either an orderly periodic sequence of stages or a random sequence of "blind" events, are not valid where chaos is found. In chaos, the innovation process engages a nonlinear dynamical system, which is neither orderly and predictable, nor stochastic and random. Learning in chaotic conditions can be viewed as an expanding and diverging process of discovery. Learning during more stable and periodic conditions is viewed as a narrowing and converging process of testing. (p. 593)

Innovation involves novelty and a voyage into the unknown (Cheng & Van de Ven, 1996). This study examines the extent to which "the seemingly-random process of innovation development may in fact not be random; it may be chaotic ...." The researchers examined data based on "conceptual categories in the learning model": continue or change in action course; positive or negative outcomes (feedback); and context events (Cheng & van de Ven, 1996, pp. 598–599). The study describes the concept of "the roughness of learning." They note:

> our research findings indicate that learning [defined as an experiential process of acquiring knowledge about action-outcome relationships and the effects of environmental events on these relationships] did not occur during the beginning period of innovation development when both action and outcome events followed a chaotic pattern, but that learning did occur after the action and outcome time series transitioned from chaotic to periodic patterns during the ending period .... This leads to the conclusion that the innovation units either learned nothing during their first four to six years of development efforts, or that they engaged in some other type of knowledge acquisition not included in the definition of learning [used in this study]. (p. 607)

Further,

> our research findings suggest that learning in chaotic conditions is an expanding and diverging process of discovering possible action alternatives, outcome preferences, and contextual settings, while learning during more stable periodic conditions is

> a narrowing and converging process of testing which actions are related to what outcomes. (p. 607)

Applying similar reasoning, Thietart and Forgues (1997) used a case study to examine the creation of context by the actions of an organization's members. They found that, "once initiated, the context tends to develop a dynamic of its own, which escapes the control of the organizational actors. *In consequence, the context becomes the determining factor of the actor's initiatives*" (p. 1, italics added). Complexity is sensitive to initial conditions, which may be why context matters so much. The study examined the well-documented Iranian hostage crisis at the American Embassy in Teheran. System dynamics were reconstructed on a daily basis to provide a "temporal description of the situation and its evolution" (Thietart & Forgues, 1997, p. 125). A total of 205 transactions were observed over a 445-day period, and were coded. To determine whether the system was chaotic, an algorithm was used employing Lyapunov exponents to determine "the time span in which the system becomes unpredictable," which is also a "measure of the rate at which the dynamic process destroys information" (Thietart & Forgues, 1997, p. 128). The researchers concluded:

> if chaos could not be eliminated by these complementary tests (that is, if chaos was likely) we would infer that what was observed in the crisis was partly constructed by the [behavior and adaptive efforts] of the actors themselves. Through their multiple actions, organizational actors create a situation which becomes impossible to control. Instead of being actors, they become subjects of a situation (chaos) which transcends their individual actions. (p. 128)

The findings of this research are consistent with those of others who consider the whole of the interacting systems and the dynamics of those interactions. Specifically, when the findings are interpreted through the principles of complexity science, the implications for learning are notable.

Themes from this review of empirical studies include:

1. context is important and determines the type of learning relied upon;
2. incidental learning helps manage the level of complexity in a given context;
3. individual actors create a chaotic context that cannot be stabilized by the same actors;
4. elapsed time is important in developing a critical mass of learning to address the level of complexity in a given context.

A notable gap is the omission of the level of complexity in the learning process, that is, the roughness of the learning process and how it emerges and abates through adaptive capacity (the ability to learn and change) and the rate of adaptiveness (how quickly emergence from learning can be applied to the given context through various forms of learning). A notable finding is that the role of incidental learning as defined by Marsick and Watkins (1990) emerges as the marginal differentiator in how chaotic environments are managed when the "protocols and procedures do not exist" for a given challenge.

INCIDENTAL LEARNING THROUGH COMPLEXITY

When learning through complexity, learners experience the white water of trying to learn rapidly enough while having to take action. Imagine you are on a sailboat and you hit turbulent waters—there is no time to take a course, consult a YouTube video, ask an expert; it's just you and the boat and the stormy waters. Like the previous studies, the study reported in Box 5.1 sought to measure how learners navigate learning under these conditions.

BOX 5.1 ROUGHNESS OF LEARNING IN UNCERTAINTY: THE ROLE OF INCIDENTAL LEARNING

Jill Karen Jinks

To develop a deeper understanding of incidental learning in a complex environment, I designed a game-based context using the serious game of Minecraft: Survival. These games are based on simple rules, yet the interactions that can manifest from the application of these rules can create edge-of-chaos effects that must be altered on some basis using the same rules that created the near chaotic state (Holland, 1998). The ability to adapt by using incidental learning in an uncertain environment was the primary focus of the research effort.

The CraftDawg Study was designed to examine the *roughness of learning* in novel contexts. Based on Marsick and Watkins' (1990) description of incidental learning, the researchers hypothesized learning in complexity is not a smooth, predictable process, but rather a rough, irregular, disorienting, confusing, and uncomfortable process. This hypothesis is based in complexity science, which accepts the irregularity of adaptive processes when systems are challenged by unexpected interventions that threaten the system's survival (Mitchell, 2009). The system adapts to meet the threat to its existence, or it dissipates. Prior learning, which influences adaptive capacity and the ability to apply that learning in novel contexts to adequately adapt, is essential for the system to sustain itself in some recognizable form.

Roughness of learning is a construct that encompasses the adaptive capacity and learning effort used to meet adaptive needs. Conceptually, it is a measure of the change in adaptive capacity and complexity associated with the intervention over various times. Simply stated: The more complex the context and the more iterative the learning effort, the greater the roughness of learning in the adaptive process. The CraftDawg study focused on (1) identifying the roughness of learning quantitatively; and (2) assessing how it changes over time as a player engages with the game over several play sessions.

In preparation for game play, participants were asked to complete three self-reported surveys. Each survey was designed to measure an element of adaptiveness as theorized from complexity science. Using ecology and environmental studies to examine adaptiveness, the researchers developed three scales to assess incidental learning, uncertainty, and adaptive capacity. These scales were used in post-play surveys completed after each play session.

An incidental learning pre-play scale was developed to assess participants' use of incidental learning methods as theorized by Marsick and Watkins (1990). Analysis of survey data revealed two forms of incidental learning—social and individual. This finding was unexpected and significant.

The researchers measured the roughness of learning variable as the composite change in incidental learning, uncertainty, and adaptiveness between plays. The roughness of learning variable is based on the perceived complexity of the learning effort. It is measured quantitatively using the game play of all the participants for each play session. For this study, five measures for each participant group were developed and compared, to assess the change in the roughness of learning between plays (within group) and between groups.

Findings

The findings of the study, as expected, showed higher roughness of learning for participants who identified as novices, and the roughness of learning decreased at a slower rate between plays. Advanced players initially had high roughness of learning, and it decreased quickly to a very low level. Intermediate players were between these two groups and showed a distinctive pattern of adaptation as measured by the change in the roughness of learning variable over the course of play. Perhaps this was the result of the advanced players being able to quickly recognize the edge-of-chaos situation where prior experience was not adequate for the new context. These players quickly adapted using their prior learning from other games. Of note, these players had low levels of uncertainty, and thus leveraged prior learning more quickly to reduce the complexity from novelty within the game. Novice players evidenced a slower adaptive process where initially the player relied on incidental learning, yet uncertainty was high and thus adaptiveness was low. Over the course of play, the novice participants adapt. Uncertainty decreases, the use of incidental learning increases, and overall adaptive processes increase. As the adaptiveness increases, the player's death rate decreases at an increasing rate. The roughness of learning begins to decrease. The player becomes more confident in strategies and tactics, and more successful.

There were significant differences in the relationships between incidental learning, uncertainty, and adaptiveness, based on the self-reported experience of the player. As expected, uncertainty was less influential with more experienced players in determining adaptiveness. Similarly, the roughness of learning (RoL) for these players was less over the course of play. There was a difference in the roughness of learning variable between the groups, with the novice group having the highest level of RoL and the slowest progression to lower levels, followed by the intermediate group, which had a lower initial roughness of learning that dropped more quickly than the novice group. The advanced group had an initially high level that dropped immediately and consistently to a low floor when compared to the other two groups.

Implications of the Study

From this study, several new paths of potential research are revealed. The finding of a social component of incidental learning is notable. Organizations have long appreciated and leveraged the use of experienced staff working with, and coaching new staff. Perhaps what has been minimized is the incidental learning that is context-specific, housed in the simple interactions overheard by others throughout the workday. This "environmental" learning that is neither sought nor offered exists incidentally. It is likely both cultural and technical in nature. With remote work models being adapted by many organizations, this type of learning may be lost.

The roughness of learning, both conceptually and as measured quantitatively, adds a dimension to incidental learning theory that opens new paths to research that assess the irregular, sometimes painful and disjointed learning that is used and developed in novel, edge-of-chaos situations. Prior research has observed and reported on these disorienting moments. This research begins to offer methods of measuring and comparing this construct in tangible and comparative ways.

In learning and development, incidental learning is rarely acknowledged. To illustrate, a participant in a workshop we conducted listened to our description of this kind of learning and commented, "That sounds like something we need to weed out!" Yet, the isolation of the pandemic, and of remote work, has made more visible how we rely on incidental learning in our daily lives.

Nancy Dixon describes both the value, and the lack of recognition for incidental learning, as the hallways of learning. She also shows how such learning is the backbone of group and organizational collaboratively derived learning culture and practices key to sustaining adaptive learning.

BOX 5.2 THE ONLY PLACE EMPLOYEES SHARE THEIR KNOWLEDGE

Nancy M. Dixon

Hallways are the places where some of our best conversations occur. Ask any conference attendee, and you're likely to hear the familiar comment, "The sessions were OK, but I had some great hallway conversations."

Why do hallway exchanges, whether at a conference center or in the workplace, have such a different feel from the events in meeting rooms and offices? Perhaps the Hallway removes some of the sense of hierarchy, making participants seem more equal. Perhaps it's because the Hallway invites multiple perspectives—anyone who wanders by can join in, adding their ideas to the mix. By the same token, perhaps people feel free to walk away if the subject proves uninteresting: Those organizational norms that require we feign interest in a topic are weaker in the Hallway. For all these reasons, we talk more freely and openly in the Hallway—perhaps we talk in more depth as well, being more willing to raise those subjects that are of concern to us but that seem undiscussable in other settings.

The Hallway is a useful analogy for talking about organizational learning. Most of the organization literature considers organizational learning as a process, or a series of processes, through which an organization constructs the meaning that guides its action. It is these learning-related processes themselves that constitute organizational learning, rather than the knowledge that is accumulated as a result of the processes. The accumulated knowledge is essential, but it is time-limited and must continually be renewed.

Knowledge renewal is critical because many of the most challenging problems organizations face are ones they have never encountered before; that are unique to a given situation. Increasingly, organizational members find that they must learn their way out of their problems—they must gather the available information and create meaning from it for themselves. Knowledge from experts or other parts of the organization may inform their thinking but cannot replace it. What is required, then, are processes that allow the organization to construct new meaning continuously; to learn.

It is helpful to consider three categories of meaning that organizational members construct: private meaning, which can be likened to Private Office space; accessible meaning, which is analogous to Hallways; and collective meaning, which corresponds to a Storeroom.

Private Office

Each individual in an organization constructs meaning for themselves. Each makes sense of what is happening in the organization, with co-workers, with customers; each attends classes, reads books, talks with experts; each plans, strategizes, and reflects. It is a continual process of constructing and re-constructing meaning as individuals encounter new experiences and ideas. Over time, each accumulates a great deal of knowledge and expertise about the organization and about their job. But even when we envision a whole organization full of individuals, each possessing extensive knowledge and expertise, we cannot be assured that the organization is learning. Each individual may keep the meaning they construct within the walls of a private office.

For example, imagine a field representative who installs and repairs the company's product and, over time, determines that a given part repeatedly fails under certain identifiable conditions. At this point, the field representative is constructing private meaning. The organization will not learn unless this private meaning is shared with others. There can, of course, be very legitimate personal reasons for individuals' keeping the meaning they construct to themselves. For example, the meaning may be about personal issues that are of little value to the organization; the meaning may have been constructed from information that would violate someone's confidence if revealed; an individual may see a personal competitive advantage in keeping the meaning quiet. Although there are understandable reasons for keeping meaning private, the more willing individuals are to make the meaning they are constructing available to others, the more the organization can learn.

Hallways

Hallways are places where ideas get tested against the thinking of others. As long as meaning is held privately, it is protected from the discovery that it may be wrong or limited in perspective. When it is made accessible to others, the data on which it is based can be challenged, and the reasoning and logic that led to the conclusions can be examined. Hallways are places where collective meaning is made. In other words, meaning is not just exchanged; it is constructed in the dialogue between organizational members. The act of one person articulating the meaning another constructed serves to clarify that meaning for both. Individuals often do not know what meaning they have made until they attempt to put it into words.

The meaning each organizational member articulates influences others. Influence does not necessarily imply agreement, but it does suggest a cognizance or recognition. Out of this confluence of ideas, new meaning develops, which no one individual brought into the Hallway. It is this joint construction of meaning that is organizational learning. What is most important about any event is not what happened but what it means. And because events and meanings are loosely coupled, the same event can have very different meanings to different people. To the extent that meaning is made privately, it remains unique to each individual; to the extent that it is constructed jointly, the organization learns. The categorical boundary between private and accessible meaning is gradual and flexible. For example, individuals may be willing to make their meaning accessible under some circumstances but not under others, or they may be willing to communicate their meaning only to select organization members. Thus, the same meaning may sometimes be private and sometimes accessible.

Storeroom

Collective meaning is like having a Storeroom where the mementos of the past are kept. These are the norms, strategies, and assumptions that specify how work gets done and what work is important to do. Collective meaning may be codified in policies and procedures, but to be collective, this meaning must also reside in the minds of organizational members. It provides a sense of belonging and community. Organizational members create the collective meaning, yet it can become so familiar that they forget they created it and begin to think it is simply the "way things are."

Collective meaning saves the organization time. There is no need for lengthy discussions about those issues that organizational members agree about—time can be spent on more critical issues. The meaning in the Storeroom can, however, have a negative impact on the organization. In a rapidly changing world, collective meaning that was advantageous at one point may have become obsolete, yet may prove difficult to change. Collective meaning makes introducing new ideas that conflict with existing meaning difficult to implement. Collective meaning is viewed by those who hold it as "truth." It is not questioned; the organization's members do not need to question what they know from long years of experience to be true.

Hallways are the only space where it is possible for an organization to learn. It cannot learn in the Private Offices, although individual learning can undoubtedly occur there. It cannot learn in the Storeroom, where it is only possible to affirm what is already known. If organizations are going to learn, they will need to construct Hallways in which the in-depth exploration of meaning can occur. The actual hallways of our organizations will not suffice for the level of organizational learning that is necessary. Instead, organizations need to develop processes that have the positive characteristics of actual hallways yet are more focused and intentional.

Many organizations have developed processes that serve this Hallway function. Some are Knowledge Management processes, such as After Action Reviews, Peer Assists, Communities of Practice, and Storytelling Circles. Others are "whole system in the room" approaches, such as Open Space Technology, Knowledge Cafés, and Appreciative Inquiry. Still others result from the rise of post-bureaucratic organizations that, by design, create more Hallway structures, for example, self-managed organizations, networked organizations, and democratic organizations, to name a few.

As varied as the current processes are, it is possible to identify common characteristics that may represent the six critical elements any such processes would need to facilitate collective meaning: (1) reliance on discussion, not speeches; (2) egalitarian participation; (3) encouragement of multiple perspectives; (4) non-expert-based database, e.g., the ideas of those in the room; and (5) creating of a shared experience. Perhaps a sixth characteristic should be added as well: (6) creating unpredictable outcomes.

The frequency of such processes in organizations, which has increased rapidly over the last few years, attests to both the need for Hallways and the ingenuity of organizations in creating new forms of collective learning.

So what does this mean for L&D practitioners? As people attempt to harness the adaptations created during the pandemic, it is clear that what was learned incidentally can be quite valuable—but it needs to be surfaced, vetted, and translated into practice. By more openly embracing incidental learning, we can begin to unleash the pragmatic imagination—to create our own design unbound (Pendleton-Jullian & Brown, 2018a). To create new knowledge, new approaches we have never imagined, learning and development will find their source in the incidental learning we engage in today.

6. Creating a learning culture

An increasingly significant action in workplace learning and development is to develop the organization, focusing on strategies to enhance organizational effectiveness. Organization development is about planned change. Richard Beckhard (2006) defined it thus: "organization development is an effort: (1) planned, (2) organization-wide, (3) managed from the top, (4) to increase organization effectiveness and health, through (5) planned interventions in the organization's processes using behavioral science knowledge" (p. 3). While leadership is increasingly more team-based, matrixed, or collective than top down as Beckhard argues, leadership is generally involved in, and supportive of, efforts to develop the organization. Burke and Litwin (1992) differentiate between transactional and transformational organizational processes, noting that, for the most part, the work of organization development is in the transformational spaces—changing organizational culture, mission and strategy, and leadership. Change in any of these dimensions can alter the whole organization. Thus the work of organization development staff is often executive development, rolling out new mission and vision initiatives, or supporting culture change efforts.

Burke and Litwin (1992) also maintain that transformational dynamics must interact with transactional dynamics—that is, those practices and systems involving implementation. As implementation occurs, it opens space for intervening transformationally; and as that transformative intervention occurs, it in turn opens space for deeper, more integrative transactional dynamics. This interaction explains why it is powerful to link organizational development (OD) with rethought learning and development (L&D)—thus rethinking the way these two approaches as interventions can more seamlessly, and integratedly, be levers for changing the boundaries of what is included in L&D and in culture or leadership change, thus making both strategies more powerful. Gephart and Marsick (2016) provide case studies that show how this interaction occurs (via practices, mechanisms, structures, etc.) through a learning approach to change—involving experimentation that is often initiated and enacted from the middle and/or grassroots levels. These initiatives were largely, if not wholly, organic and not guided by OD. Thus, the role of L&D is to nurture and jumpstart experimentation, but also to identify and grow naturally occurring learning for change.

WATKINS AND MARSICK MODEL

In our work, we focus on creating a learning culture. Adding complexity science to the mix, along with a focus on learning, means organization development is no longer necessarily managed from the top, nor rational or as deliberate as these early scholars envisioned. In our view, organization development is closer to action research—an evidence-based evolutionary process of learning our way through the inevitable complexities that arise when we change human systems (Marsick & Watkins, 1996). While other definitions focused on strategies of deliberate changing of systems (Bennis et al., 1969), Argyris (1970) focused on the organization developer and the interventions themselves, which he defined as "to come between and among systems for the purpose of helping them" (p. 15). Our view resonates with Argyris', whose ethical stance permeates his theory—that essentially the organization developer must do no harm. And to do no harm, they need to have valid information and the client needs to have free and informed choice about whether or not to make a change, as well as internal commitment to that choice.

For Argyris (1976), the process of change proceeded through recurring cycles of diagnosis, invention of a response to the diagnosis, producing the invention in a real setting, and finally generalization of the solution to other situations. Argyris noted that the problem is that we cannot always enact what we can imagine. We have to learn how to enact what we have proposed. And, at times, what we proposed is not feasible nor is it the better solution, hence we need to modify our beliefs and adjust our actions. This is where Lewin's (1946) model of action research is at the heart of effective OD practice.

Lewin (1946) called for a new form of research to guide social action he called "action research." He suggested that change begins with a reconnaissance of the current situation, which then leads to a general plan of how to proceed. Lewin emphasized that you need to remain open and flexible to respond to what is learned at each stage of the change process. Through iterative cycles of researching the situation, taking action, collecting data on the action taken, revising the action (or rethinking and reframing the problem) based on the new data, the problem may ultimately be addressed. Data are essential to confirm or question the nature of the problem, or challenge the system faces, but they also serve as a potential way to unfreeze a stuck system. By seeing the gap between where the organization is now and where it wants to be, others may recognize the need to change and join the change effort. Our model of organization development acknowledges these perspectives, integrating a social collaborative approach with one that emphasizes learning is essential to implementation. Figure 6.1 gives our model of learning and change.

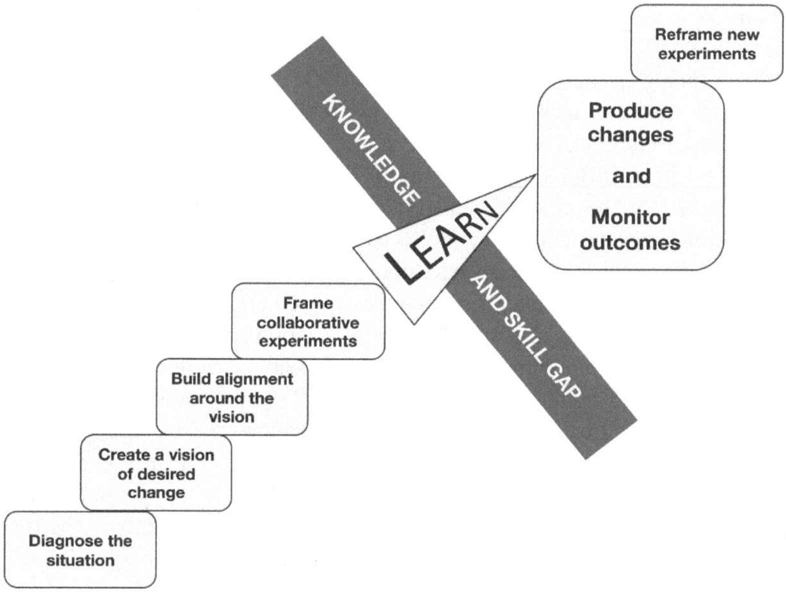

Source: Adapted from Marsick and Watkins, 1999.

Figure 6.1 Marsick and Watkins' integrated learning and change model

All change involves learning, yet change management strategies often assume leaders can mandate a change and employees will simply adopt that change with no training or support. In our model, we envision framing collaborative experiments: the iterative process of trying something out with a team of interested stakeholders, looking for small wins that move the organization toward its intended vision, followed by reflection on what was learned in this attempt and what is needed next to continue movement toward the vision. Ours is a learning approach to change, one that, as in complexity science (and in Lewin), is emergent and continuously adapting to the context and what is learned along the way.

Theory U

There are similarities to Scharmer's Theory U (2009). Scharmer asked, "How do you learn and lead in times of disruption when you cannot rely on the experiences of the past?" He envisioned a U-shaped process that began with downloading and unlearning prior expectations and beliefs to enable an opening of the mind to possibilities—engaging the pragmatic imagination

(Pendleton-Jullian & Brown, 2018b)—followed by small experiments or prototyping, from which the future state may emerge. Scharmer works from an ecological perspective—complex adaptive systems and a mindfulness focus on being in the present, "presencing." Scharmer and colleagues at the Presencing Institute tackle huge, systemic problems, such as working from a problem at Starbucks around coffee supplies, to following the supply chain to work with the coffee farmers in South America supplying the coffee beans. They argue that the precarity and failure of many of our systems "call for a new consciousness and a new collective leadership capacity to meet these challenges in a more conscious, intentional, and strategic way."[1] In Scharmer's model, change is undertaken collaboratively—co-creating, co-initiating, etc. This is again similar to action research where action research teams engage in cycles of action (prototyping, co-creating) and team reflection (co-sensing).

The Presencing Institute has developed a number of tools to help leaders build these capacities, such as stakeholder interviews, case studies, learning journeys, prototyping, etc., as well as certification for awareness-based systems change. Moving from a more individual or organizational mindset to a more ecological mindset invites leaders to look more deeply at the roots and ramifications of the problems they hope to solve by instituting a proposed change. Senge's (1997) conception of a learning organization also zeroed in on the critical importance of systems thinking to creating organizations that can learn and survive, calling it the fifth discipline.

Adapting to Environmental Jolts

Complexity theory stresses the interdependence of systems as well as their complex adaptability and self-organization at the edge of chaos (Murray, 1998). A classic study of environmental jolts by Meyer (1982) illustrates this complex adaptability. Meyer studied how 19 hospitals responded to a doctors' strike. Noting that a minor earthquake rarely topples buildings and smaller jolts do not threaten well-designed organizations that are aligned with their environment, Meyer points out that more seismic tremors can not only topple buildings but can also expose hidden flaws in architecture and construction in buildings—and in organizations (p. 515). Meyer found that "the impacts of jolts are influenced by strategies and absorbed by slack resources; the reactions to jolts are shaped by ideologies and constrained by structures" (p. 529). Organizational ideologies determined whether or not the jolt was interpreted as a dilemma, an aberration, or an opportunity. This collective meaning making led to strategies that attempted either to return as soon as possible to things as they were before the strike or to seize the opportunity to adapt and create new strategies and structures. Declines in measures of occupancy, employment, and revenue were smallest in hospitals that were well connected to their environments, supported "strategic reorientations, embraced organizational changes, valued members' capabilities, and encouraged participation" (p. 531). Meyer found that organizational learning was enhanced by entrepreneurial and adaptive strategies, and by a structure that diffused decision making. These findings mirror the experience of many organizations in attempting to rebound from the pandemic.

Meyer's work influenced our understanding of a learning organization—an organization with the capacity to transform itself (Watkins & Marsick, 1993). Our initial work began with a deep dive into the organizational change literature, looking at how organizations could be transformed to support continuous change—how they could learn to be more agile and more adept at implementing innovations (Watkins and Marsick, 1993, 1996; Marsick and Watkins, 1999). Lundberg (1989) argued that the idea of the learning organization may "upwing the distance vision of organization development" (p. 62). We agree. By shaping the organization itself to be more open and responsive to change, the implementation of individual change initiatives would presumably be smoother. More importantly, the idea of a learning organization recognizes that all change involves learning. Ultimately, we defined a learning organization as one that has a greater capacity to learn and to change (Watkins & Marsick, 1993). Watkins and Kim (2018) summarize how the seven dimensions of a learning organization change the culture and capacity of the organization:

> Organizations structured to promote continuous learning have a culture that provides an infrastructure rich with resources and tools for individuals to engage in formal and especially informal learning. It facilitates and encourages dialogue and inquiry at all levels. Systems are in place to capture suggestions for change and lessons learned. The culture emphasizes team learning and a spirit of collaboration in order to promote cross-unit learning. Central to the culture is that it empowers people to enact a collective vision and makes systemic connections between the organization and its environment, scanning the environment to learn and anticipate future needs. Leadership is transformed as well. A learning culture provides leadership for learning through leaders who facilitate the development of their employees and engage in learning themselves (Marsick & Watkins, 2003; Watkins & Marsick, 1993, 1996). (Watkins & Kim, 2018, p. 19)

Central to our vision of rethinking learning and development is that the organization's culture itself needs to be wired for learning and change. This moves organization development beyond short term initiatives to embedding adaptive capacities in the organization. In the complexity that organizations face today, planned change is a luxury, and it is often compounded by multiple concurrent change activities. Change fatigue is common. A learning approach focuses on tapping into organizational reserves and building skills of organization members to implement change. Empowerment and alignment with the culture and the organization's purpose and mission ensures that organization members, even when making independent decisions, will make them in a manner that furthers organizational visions. The dimensions in our model collectively and interdependently create the systems that open the organization to learn and to innovate. The culture, in turn, is enacted and reinforced by new practices, structures, management, and communication systems, etc.

Hagel III et al. (2010) add insight to how an ecological perspective builds capacity for fulfilling the vision that the learning organization initially offered—what Senge (1990) described as:

> organizations where people continually expand their capacity to create the results they truly desire, where new and expansive patterns of thinking are nurtured, where collective aspiration is set free, and where people are continually learning to see the whole together. (p. 3)

Hagel III et al. (2010) describe creation spaces that exist outside the boundaries of organizations through "ecosystems across institutions ... [that] reach a much more diverse set of participants" and are driven by "their goal ... to drive more rapid performance improvement ... [in which] learning occurs as a byproduct of these efforts," thus echoing the rising importance of incidental learning in complex circumstances. Creation spaces are powered by intrinsic motivation (purpose), collaboration, and the joy of achieving higher levels of mastery through dynamic peer interaction.

Dimensions of a Learning Organization Questionnaire

Over time, the seven action imperatives we developed from our research as critical to creating a more adaptive organization were also operationalized in a survey, the Dimensions of a Learning Organization Questionnaire (DLOQ) (Watkins and Marsick, 1997). Our survey has now been used in over a hundred studies in more than twenty languages around the world. Consistently, the instrument has proved to be not only reliable but also highly correlated with organizational performance (Ellinger et al., 2002; Ju et al., 2021; Watkins & Dirani, 2013), especially knowledge performance. Ellinger et al. (2002) found that over a quarter of the variance in knowledge and financial performance was accounted for by the seven dimensions of a learning organization using our perceptual measures. Using objective financial performance measures, 10% of the variance was accounted for by the seven dimensions. It is astounding—given the many factors influencing financial performance—that these dimensions correlate positively and have a significant impact. This finding has important implications for learning and development because knowledge performance is the intellectual capital, the innovativeness of an organization, and this is the organizational performance metric most influenced by learning and development.

Kaplan and Norton (1992) developed the balanced scorecard that looked at how an organization's intangible assets help project long-term financial performance. As Hoque (2014) notes, "Kaplan and Norton introduced the idea of combining financial and non-financial (customer, internal business, and innovation and learning) perspectives in a single performance scorecard model, the Balanced Business Scorecard" (p. 35). Kaplan and Norton believed that intangible assets were causally related to financial assets. Around the same time, Beck (1992), a Canadian economist, was developing a way of tracking these non-financial assets to identify investment opportunities. Beck's approach was to find something to track that would be an advance indicator that an organization's intangible assets were growing. For example, to look at innovation, she would track sales of the platforms that companies used to ship computers. Our approach to measuring knowledge performance in the DLOQ drew on Kaplan and Norton and Beck's approaches.

LEADERSHIP FOR LEARNING

People have correlated transformational versus transactional leadership with our dimensions of a learning organization, to see if either made a significant difference. These authors generally drew on Bass and Avolio's (1989) conception of transactional leadership as a contingent reward or exchange-based approach to leadership, as contrasted with transformational leadership, which leads through vision, and often charisma, as embodied in their Multifactor Leadership Questionnaire (MLQ). Lang (2013) found that transactional styles in Cambodian banks had more influence in cultivating a learning organization. Pimapunsri (2014) found that transformational leadership styles were highly correlated with dimensions of a learning organization—though only three dimensions were used in the study: dialogue and inquiry, embedded systems, and providing strategic leadership for learning—across frontline subordinates from 13 companies in Thailand. Carter (2016) found a strong correlation between transformational leadership and the dimensions of a learning organization in hospitals, based on a sample of board-certified perioperative nurses. Comparing the impact of servant leadership and transformational leadership on the learning organization, Xie (2020) found that servant leadership had no significant impact while transformational leadership had significant impact in a study of full-time employees in two small and medium-size enterprises. Looking across these widely disparate settings, leadership for transformation appears to support creating a learning culture.

In our research, providing strategic leadership for learning is the most significant of the seven dimensions (Kim & Watkins, 2018). It correlates with both knowledge and financial performance. Like transformational leadership, our leadership dimension is focused on leading learning and change. Within the leadership dimension, the most significant item was that leaders mentor and coach those they lead (Kim & Watkins, 2018). This informal learning approach and the leaders' role in facilitating this learning signals a significant shift in how learning happens in the organization and who leads that learning. Ellinger and Bostrom (2002) explore the differing approaches leaders take to facilitate the learning of their employees and note that leaders in learning organizations have to resolve their belief that coaching and managing are dichotomous. Whatever the approach, the bottom line is that for leaders and managers, facilitating learning now has to be part of their portfolio, and L&D professionals can help them both direct and monitor behavior, while also providing helpful coaching on how employees can improve their behavior.

CREATING A LEARNING CULTURE

What does it look like when L&D and OD personnel approach their work from a learning culture perspective? One example comes from Tonya Cornileus, formerly Vice President of Development, Inclusion and Wellness, at ESPN/Disney, and currently Senior Vice President of Learning and Talent Solutions for the Walt Disney Company. Dr. Cornileus managed both L&D and organization development in her portfolio, and thus was able to integrate across both functions in key initiatives. Note how the learning initiatives were also cultural initiatives and, at the same time, sensemaking opportunities that triggered additional support and leadership responses.

BOX 6.1 INCLUSIVE CONVERSATIONS—EVERY VOICE MATTERS

Tonya Cornileus, Vice President of Development, Inclusion and Wellness, ESPN/Disney

I believe people learn in small groups that are in conversation with one another. We have a culture where people like to meet. The café on our campus in Bristol, for example, buzzes. It's the hub, the nerve center of the campus, because people come there and they meet, eat, and have conversations. People love to come together and have discussions and dialogue. We thought, "That's cultural for us." So we started Inclusive Conversations based on the belief that "Every Voice Matters." It was a part of a Diversity, Equity, and Inclusion (DEI) initiative, but it was also a learning initiative. We catered lunches where people are sitting around the table almost living-room style, breaking bread together. When we first started, there were questions at the table such as, "What is inclusion? What does that mean to you? When have you experienced it? When have you not felt included? How inclusive is ESPN [a sports media company owned by Disney] and what is one thing we could do to be a more inclusive culture?" The inclusive conversations started with trying to define inclusion and the employee experience of inclusion.

Certainly we were on to something because people were signing up and there were waitlists. Then the pandemic happened. We started facilitating conversations around what they were going through, and we provided links to just-in-time resources for them and their family members, and things like that. Then George Floyd was murdered. The Inclusive Conversations organically sparked around social justice issues. We always envisioned that the conversations would be employee-led and cover topics that mattered most to them, and as we were all dealing with the pandemic and social issues, that's exactly what happened.

Before the pandemic, I don't think leaders spent a lot of time checking on their employees' well-being beyond "How are you doing?" What we heard through these conversations is that if employees had a leader who opened a meeting saying, "Let's check in with one another first," that made the employee feel this sense of belonging and that the company cared for them. We coached our leaders around storytelling: How do you tell stories of your own vulnerability so you create a safe space, an inclusive environment for others to be able to share? Those things evolve culture. And the role of the leader is paramount in setting the tone for the culture. You can take what you gather from these conversations and make real change in leadership. You can make real change in culture.

Initially, Disney started what they called Safe Space conversations in reaction to the MeToo movement. They were creating the space for employees to share and be open, and to be heard. From a DEI perspective, that's truly important in building an inclusive culture. They introduced me to a model from an outside firm, Civic Dinners, that would host dinners for citizens of a company or community and invite them to meet around the dinner table on a topic. I liked components of that model because it's cultural to ESPN—finding what is cultural to us, not teeing it up as a reaction to a problem, and asking how we leverage these components to foster greater dialogue within our culture led to our approach. These are employee-driven conversations. Our nine employee resource groups are the main leaders of these conversations. They can be around a topic that matters to that dimension of diversity or to the broader employee population.

In our first meeting we had 40 to 50 people in an intimate setting with just eight people around round tables. The environment matters. We wanted them to have a beginning topic, but they could add topics. There was a facilitator at the table, but facilitating lightly. There was a flip chart at each table. We had them in a huge room and the facilities team set up lunch settings that looked like you're going out to lunch with a group. The conversations started as a large group to explain what we were doing and why, and answered any questions people had. They were randomly assigned to a group; the group then went to their space, which was partitioned off so everyone had some privacy. They had a little over an hour to have lunch and talk about the topic and whatever other topics came up. At the end, people came back and shared what they had learned and noted on the flip chart key ideas about inclusion, including what the company could do to create a more inclusive culture.

When the pandemic hit, we moved to Zoom. We weren't sure people would attend because you have this technological barrier. You're not around a table. But people still participated. We had maybe half a dozen or so conversations prior to the pandemic. Over the course of the pandemic, we have had close to a hundred.

We don't record the conversations, but we do keep the chat. There are questions we pose at the beginning and then we circle back at the end. We capture the answers to those questions. During the pandemic, when we were addressing COVID-19 and their anxieties around the pandemic, the focus was, "How are you feeling today? What are you uncertain about? What support do you need?" We captured the answers and that helped us know what resources to start funneling out to employees. For example, they wanted to know how to access the mental well-being toolkit.

Our LGBTQIA employee resource group, EQUAL, led an inclusive conversation following the Florida legislation known as "Don't Say Gay." We had over 500 people attend that conversation, from senior leaders to entry-level employees. It was a great showing of support for our LGBTQIA employees. With the murders of George Floyd and other Black citizens flooding the news, our Black employee resource group, PULSE, held several inclusive conversations around how they were feeling. We would get questions on how to be a better ally, so we directed resources to our employees on being an ally. How do you show support? How do you not be a bystander?

Leaders would ask for resources to hold these conversations with their teams, so a person from my team had a workshop for leaders on how to facilitate these kinds of meetings within their own small groups. So, inclusive conversations evolved over time from being this DEI-driven initiative, "We're going to understand inclusion," to responding to things that are top of mind for our employees and the employee resource groups leading those conversations. Inclusive conversations have become cultural to ESPN over these two-and-a-half years. It is now just part of the lingo, "Oh, we're having an inclusive conversation."

Culture of Career

In a similar vein, I'm leading a Disney-wide project team called "Culture of Career." We are launching a new HR system that will provide leaders and employees at all levels with greater transparency and greater empowerment. Employees and leaders would have more information at their fingertips than they've ever had before; information that they usually have to go to their HR business partner to find.

This tool allows employees to create their own profiles. They will have access to their salary range, to other roles, and to what those salary ranges and grade levels are. Leaders will be able to see talent, so if they have a role and want to know who in the organization has the skills they need, it will be there. They won't have to go to Talent Acquisition to get that information. It's like an internal LinkedIn, where employees create their own employee profiles, their skills, their backgrounds, their interests, and they are searchable. Not only can they see roles, but hiring leaders can see the profiles and then say, "Hey, I want to interview these three people." How do we prepare the organization for this kind of change? How do we prepare leaders when an employee comes to them and says, "Why am I only at this salary when the range is this?" Information that was not visible before will be more visible, and we need to prepare leaders to have those difficult conversations. While the new system brings change, everyone is excited about giving leaders and employees direct access to information and empowering them to make decisions for their teams and for their careers.

Whether creating inclusive conversations or a culture of career, the role of L&D is both to anticipate the cultural impact of these interventions and to learn from them. This recursive approach ensures that L&D is responsive to the needs of the organization while also pulling it into a more inclusive future.

NOTE

1. https://www.u-school.org/theory-u (accessed March 13, 2023).

7. Teaming to innovate

Much research conducted on teams assumes they are relatively stable units with clear boundaries, common goals, and collective responsibility for results (Hackman, 1990). Complexity changes the make-up of teams, how they work together, whether or not they are co-located, and other conditions that call for rethinking teamwork and team learning. This chapter examines practices teams engage, sometimes organically and sometimes intentionally, when engaged in innovation in rapidly changing, complex environments. In so doing we examine, in particular, what Pendleton-Jullian and Brown (2018a) identify as changes at and to the boundaries of systems. Through taking new action, new learning is stimulated. Learners are crossing boundaries—made easier by the networked ecosystems in which they work and the dismantling of hierarchical, siloed models of governance. Practices stimulate, and sometimes structure, creative inquiry, perspective taking, and dialogue that opens the imagination and results in experimenting with new behaviors and actions (Gherardi, 2000).

We begin by exploring how teams and team learning are being rethought—including (1) a ground-breaking shift from teams as structures to teaming as process (Edmondson, 2012, 2013); (2) teaming as complex adaptive systems; and (3) examples of how leadership and development is being rethought in teaming to address complexity. We discuss examples of what this looks like, drawing on both the literature and research on practice. We conclude with implications for rethinking in teaming and how complexity affects such learning.

TEAMING AS PROCESS

Edmondson (2012, 2013) and Edmondson with Harvey (2017, 2018) broke new ground in rethinking teams, their cross-boundary interactions, and the role of the leader in facilitating their teams' learning. Edmondson and Harvey (2017, p. xviii) note, "a great deal of collaborative work occurs outside of formal teams entailing learning across boundaries." They shift the focus from stable team structures to processes of "teaming"—defined as:

> what happens when people collaborate—across boundaries of expertise, hierarchy, or geographic distance, to name a few. Teaming is a process of bringing together skills and ideas from disparate areas to produce something new—something

> that no one individual, or even a group in one area of expertise, could do alone. (Edmondson, 2013, p. 1)

Edmondson further contrasts differences in teaming for routine, complex, or innovative operations as teams encounter greater complexity while innovating. Extreme complexity calls for extreme teaming (Edmondson & Harvey, 2017) that requires crossing boundaries caused by deep semantic, interpersonal, and technical knowledge divides that are challenging to navigate and negotiate. When consequences, risks, and success factors cannot be fully identified,

> [t]he success of these projects depends on learning—that is, on the ability to adapt rapidly and efficiently to new knowledge. In the absence of past experience and knowledge, such projects must make recourse to learning to shape their responses to threats and opportunities. Each project participant lacks not only a body of project-specific knowledge but also contextual knowledge about viable paths to success. As a result, such projects shift rapidly in ways that are difficult or even impossible to predict. (Edmondson & Harvey, 2017, p. xix)

Edmondson and Harvey (2017) note that digital connectivity, along with other drivers, has changed the unit of analysis for work and learning. Silos and rigid organizational boundaries have given way to networked ecosystems. Edmondson and Harvey (2017) emphasize, "the success of many companies is interdependent with (rather than at odds with) that of other firms in an ecosystem" (p. 11). Specialization has given way to seeing "organizations as part of innovation systems, which support the development of knowledge between several diverse actors" (p. 13). These authors focus on leadership as a leverage point for innovation under these conditions. Leaders can rethink team learning by aiming high, teaming up, failing well, and learning fast (Edmondson, 2013).

TEAMING AS COMPLEX ADAPTIVE SYSTEMS

Collaboration and teaming are central to Watkins and Marsick's (1993) conceptualization of the learning organization. They included team learning items in the Dimensions of the Learning Organization Questionnaire (DLOQ) (see Chapter 6) drawn from Team Learning Survey research (Kasl et al., 1997) from two case studies: one across teams in a petrochemical company undergoing widespread business transformation; and the other within an IT group in manufacturing that reorganized as self-managing teams. Using grounded theory, the researchers developed a team learning model that highlights the dynamic process dimensions of team learning where members crossed boundaries to gain new perspectives, knowledge objects, or points of view—followed by questioning their earlier framing of the situation. Through conversation they reconciled different views and integrated perspectives. They could then reframe their views and try out new approaches, behaviors, and initiatives.

Our team learning model (Dechant et al., 1993) is one of several frameworks drawn on by Decuyper et al. (2010) to develop an integrative team learning model based on General Systems Theory (GST) and complexity theory:

> Both theories emphasize a shift in thinking from seeing parts to seeing the organization of parts, recognizing that the interactions of those parts are not static and constant, but dynamic processes .... [They] see teams as complex open systems with their temporal, socio-cultural, physical, economical and organisational supra-system (environment). (Decuyper et al., 2010, p. 112)

The resulting integrative model examines interrelationships rather than component elements, and embraces an interdisciplinary approach to team learning. They emphasize learning-intensive practices: "When it comes to team learning, dialogue, feedback, sharing of information, framing, reframing, confrontation, negotiation, etc., are all crucial communicative actions (Dechant et al., 1993; Edmondson, 1999)," cited in Decuyper et al. (2010, p. 116). Facilitating processes "that give context and focus to team learning" include team reflexivity, boundary crossing, and team activity (Decuyper et al., 2010, p. 117) involving implicit and explicit learning by doing.

Experimentation is "highly important to test the group's cognitive hypotheses, shared mental models and decisions in practice, or to discover and assess their impact" (Decuyper et al., 2010, p. 118). Both planned and unplanned activity are valued for different reasons. "Unplanned/chaotic team activity may lead to disrupting experiences or creative boosts" (Arrow et al., 2000; Homan, 2001, as cited by Decuyper et al., 2010, p. 118). Disruption in highly complex circumstances leads to questioning and experimentation to probe and learn. There are no clear answers and there is great value in identifying important questions.

Boundary Crossing

Decuyper et al. (2010) call out boundary crossing, as do both Kasl et al. (1997) and Edmondson (2012, 2013). Decuyper et al. (2010) define boundaries as "the intangible but very real lines which separate person from person, group from group, and group from organization" and further define boundary crossing as "to seek or give information, views, and ideas through interaction with other individuals or units"; noting that such boundaries can be "physical, mental, or organizational" (p. 118). Boundary crossing is especially important given that altering a complex system's boundaries is a gateway to changing the course of events and is often the locus for creativity and invention for "design unbound" in complex adaptive systems (Pendleton-Jullian and Brown, 2018b).

Robbins (2020, p. 1), for example, in a comparison across five seed-phase entrepreneurial teams in a business school incubator, found that successful teams used "tools like turn taking, probing, and repair (error correction or gradual refinement—by self or other) ... for dealing with conflict" (p. 15). Less successful teams were "less likely ... to describe high levels of communication and dialogue" (p. 14). The teams as systems could, but did not always, alter the boundaries set by knowledge barriers—e.g., language, interpretations, and interests (Edmondson and Harvey, 2018). Yet, they might use tools and protocols that open and alter boundaries, thus serving as mechanisms for learning through and with complexity.

Decuyper et al. (2010) note the importance of Edmondson's findings that team psychological safety mediates between empowering leadership of the positional leader and learning capacity. They point to the value of considering leadership in a functional way, the choice Edmondson (2013) also makes when discussing extreme teaming and complexity:

> [A functionalist approach] no longer involves the tripod "leaders – followers – shared goals," because it shifts the focus from the question "who is the leader?" or "what should the leader do?" to "what needs to be done?" Team leadership is then defined in terms of the conditions or functions that need to be present in a team, in order to be learning and working effectively .... Defining leadership in a functionalist way also opens the possibility of conceptualizing leadership as "shared." (Decuyper et al., 2010, p. 125)

Cross-Functional Teaming in Regulated Knowledge Environments

In the following vignette (Box 7.1), Elizabeth Robinson (2021) shares her research examining a cross-functional team (using pseudonyms) that incorporated a new type of data visualization technology into an educational video for healthcare professionals. The team worked in a scientific communications agency that partners with healthcare clients to provide consulting and support to pharmaceutical, biopharmaceutical, and medical diagnostic/device companies. Their educationally oriented products help healthcare professionals make informed decisions about patient treatment. These agencies might, for example, convene advisory boards, develop educational resources for a client's internal experts or sales representatives, or create disease-education programs and product-specific education for healthcare professionals. Cross-functional teams engaging in this work might include advanced degree scientists, creative and digital experts, and account service representatives.

The team described here called for both collaboration and experimentation with new ways of working, and for decentralized, shared leadership. This was the first time a dynamic form of data visualization was being used in this way. The agency strategically identified promising innovations and found client partners willing to experiment. They provided financial allowances to support first implementations, and recognized that experimentation required additional time and budget. This was a strategic investment to help learn its way into new ways of working. The team was not expected to follow standard project work formats. This study explored what crossing boundaries and shared leadership look like in this context.

BOX 7.1 CROSS-FUNCTIONAL TEAMING FOR INNOVATION WITHIN A SPECIALIZED AND REGULATED INDUSTRY

Elizabeth Robinson, Ed.D., Executive Vice President, Talent Development & Engagement, Healthcare Consultancy Group

This project was the first time that a dynamic form of data visualization had been used in an otherwise well-established format for educational communications videos. The team recognized that the innovative aspect of the project created unknowns for implementation—they would have to discover the best options. But because they were innovating, the team also experienced a sense of freedom to make mistakes, to ask questions, and to learn. Without calling it such, many team members perceived a sense of psychological safety (Edmondson, 2012)—articulated best by the two day-to-day leads, Ryan and Raveena. Ryan said, because they were doing something new, "it was not that we were making a mistake. We were just trying out a different way of doing things." Raveena also felt that, because this was new territory, when things went wrong, "you're less hard on yourself." She felt it was "a good team to do something innovative because you feel that they've got your back."

Experimentation

Although it did not alleviate all tensions that arose during experimentation, this sense of freedom to make mistakes and speak up with ideas served the team well as it geared up to plan for, and execute, the video "shoot." One of the first experiments the team undertook was to set up the mock shoot. This not only gave the team a prototype video, but it also revealed some of the challenges it would face. These pivotal learnings helped the team decide to use props during the shoot so the featured medical expert would have a sense of the scale and location of the visuals he would need to suggest in his physical movements. The mock shoot revealed the challenge of shooting the video in the customary way, based on the sequence of the script. Instead, they had to follow the order of the different camera angles needed. Following the mock shoot, the video producer described how he was compelled to speak up and advocate for using what he saw as this essential, though complex, new process. Another new process the team implemented was to convene a full-day rehearsal in advance of the shoot. This would be crucial to allow for any additional experimentation with the props and to better plan for the sequence in order of camera shots. Despite the additional preparation, the team was unprepared for the full impact that shooting the video in out-of-script order would have during the actual shoot, in part because it required following different versions of the script. It created, as Raveena said, their "biggest scramble." The climate of psychological safety was especially important during that confusion. Several team members discussed how everyone quickly focused on creating a solution versus placing any blame. That allowed them to get back on track from a schedule perspective and seemed to contribute to a positive mood and a productive shoot. The experience also generated many additional learnings for how to shoot out of sequence more smoothly going forward. As Ryan said, "That was a learning experience."

Changes in Roles and Practices

In terms of the team's operating principles, some roles and responsibilities became more fluid, while new, less formalized communications processes evolved. Team members talked about communicating more frequently via ad hoc, full-team meetings, just "getting everyone in a room" instead of dividing into sub-specialty groupings. Departing from custom, all team members were put on all communications so that, as Raveena said, "No one was sort of siloed or left out of the loop when it came time to fully executing on this project." This created an opportunity for team members to integrate perspectives and to know that their perspectives were, as a junior science team member said, "welcomed, regardless of role." While functional and level expertise was still valued and necessary, having everyone rapidly and consistently informed helped to break down functional knowledge boundaries. They learned they needed to all be on the same page at the same time. They needed to collectively share information, discuss progress/barriers, and make decisions about how to proceed next. All members needed to weigh in; everyone's perspective and support was critical. The team thus created new protocols for shared communication, for example, including everyone in all email communications, and convening frequent unscheduled full-team meetings to process new information and discoveries and align on next steps.

These innovation-responsive operating principles contributed to effective crossing of boundaries and collaboration, both of which facilitated the team's learning and performance. The act of working collaboratively resulted in greater learning than if they worked alone. While collaboration was essential for all cross-functional teaming, it was especially critical for innovation. It guided how the team chose to take new actions as well as how everyone freely generated ideas. The overall team lead, Sharon, stated that no one person was "in charge of the thinking"; rather, it was very collaborative. Another mid-level client service team member felt people "found their voice," which enabled them to "speak up about what the process should be, what they saw that could be different." This level of collaboration led to the team's ability to work together almost as a single unit, especially during the critical shoot day. As Allegra said, by that time they had learned to navigate unexpected challenges, and the team members were "gelling together" so well that the experience of that day was "perfect."

Shared Team Leadership

Just as the team's operating principles and behaviors adapted to respond to the innovative aspect of the project, so did its model of leadership. Sharon was the main point of contact for the client, though other senior staff from the creative, science, and digital functions guided key decisions and client discussions. As the work progressed, these senior leaders began to disperse more authority to the mid- and junior-level staff. As a junior science team member said, they wanted to "empower our hands-on team to figure out how to make this work." Ultimately, it was the more junior science and account team members, Ryan and Raveena, who partnered to lead the team daily with support from the mid-level creative and digital team members. These team members described this approach to leadership as collaborative and shared, with every member's expertise valued and leveraged at different times. Being less experienced, these team members were less entrenched in established processes and seemed comfortable and excited to figure out the best way to approach the innovative aspects of the project. Allegra noted they were not "freaked out," but saw this project as an "exciting opportunity … to do the very first dynamic visualization video for the client and our agency."

Team Learning Outcomes

This team was the first to implement this new type of video. Team members described it as a major accomplishment, a great showpiece, and a template for future work. Its key process learnings centered on the intricacies of the choreography and the need to plan out all of the medical expert's interactions with the graphics. The team recognized how these learnings could make the process more efficient, how it could help others to "hit the ground running," and, as Monique said, how it could help others to not default to a traditional approach when "being a little untraditional is more beneficial in this case." The team figured out new ways of working and, at the conclusion of the study, were already beginning to share some of its learnings informally with another team that was about to implement this same type of project.

From Team to Organizational Learning

This team's ability to learn and perform depended on the way in which the organization committed to innovation, which included empowering the team to experiment with different approaches to support the innovative technical aspect of the project. They also provided forums for the team to share their learnings with other teams across the organization, many of whom adopted these emerging practices as they implemented this new kind of educational video for their clients.

This vignette illustrates emergent practices. The challenge to the scientific communications agency lies in how to draw on this experiment in crossing boundaries—recognizing that, with complexity, the next set of circumstances an innovation team might face will not be exactly the same. How can leaders and organizations adopt and adapt the flexible, adaptable learning approach demonstrated here without turning it into a checklist or rigid protocol for future teams whose circumstances and composition might call for alternative approaches to boundary crossing in future scenarios? One way of doing so is to better understand the dynamics of practices that support learning, so to speak, in the workflow of teaming. The next section explores learning-intensive work practices to provide structure and scaffolding for team learning.

PRACTICES THAT SUPPORT TEAM LEARNING IN COMPLEXITY

Gherardi (2000) noted that, "in everyday practices, learning takes place in the flow of experience, with or without our awareness of it. In everyday organizational life, work, learning, innovation, communication, negotiation, conflict over goals, their interpretation, and history, are co-present in practice" (p. 214). Practice is both production and "product of specific historical conditions" (p. 215) that evolve organically over time, and are subject to conservative forces of socialization into "how we do things around here." Gherardi argues that practice studies help us to understand both how practices socialize, but also, the way they disrupt. Cultural-historical development theory speaks to this dialectical tension (status quo versus innovation) (Scully-Russ & Boyle, 2018). Vygotsky (1978) spoke to breaking out of the status quo to complete historical potential for cultural growth and development—that is, innovation. Change can be gradual. However, as Edmondson and Harvey (2017) note, tools can be introduced to facilitate learning and experimentation. In some circumstances, the intervention itself is intended to use disruption to intervene in the system. Learning while teaming is thus rethought and redesigned to center inquiry, experimentation, and reframing.

Several interventions illustrate what complex adaptive systems (CAS) practices of this kind might look like when seeking to alter the boundaries of a system and influence the opening up of multiple perspectives and the building of the imagination muscle (Pendleton-Jullian and Brown, 2018b). These interventions echo some of the tools described in *Design Unbound*, such as expanding the brief by continued inquiry into the multiple layers and stakeholders involved in any situation in order to open new thinking about framing the situation and context. Pendleton-Jullian and Brown speak to learning in the face of ambiguity—often in its natural occurrences but also at times through interventions that deliberately structure ambiguity into the learning process to generate and consider alternatives. "*Orchestrating ambiguity* is the guiding of multiple ambiguities into an ensemble that creates a chord of meaning that conveys a specific complex melody, harmony, or story" (Pendleton-Jullian & Brown, 2018a, p. 135). Facilitators act as orchestra directors, "weaving different tones and characteristics of individual instruments into a composition" (p. 135). We explore two of these learning and development (L&D) examples: FlowTeam Design to engage multiple stakeholders in expanding the brief, and relying on agile practices to implicitly structure learning through rapid iteration.

FlowTeam Design

FlowTeams are guided by an animator aided by practices, dynamics, and structures designed to be learner-centric and learner-controlled. The process stimulates the imagination and engages diverse participants in open-ended inquiry—using cognitive equity and imagination, as Pendleton-Jullian and Brown (2018a) suggest—to address complexity. In this example, FlowTeams are used to surface and explore different points of view in the presence of ambiguity due to multiple actors' perspectives in a global semiconductor design and manufacturing organization. In doing so, entangled layers of views and competing priorities are explored so new solutions can emerge. Bill Gardner, an internal L&D consultant, tells the story.

BOX 7.2 FLOWTEAMS—A COMPLEX ADAPTIVE SYSTEMS APPROACH TO STRATEGIC TEAMS

William (Bill) Gardner, Founder and Managing Partner, Noetic Outcomes Consulting, LLC

Martin Gerber—at the time an organization development (OD) director of a global manufacturing organization—had grown skeptical of "a popular interest in 'management by recipe.'" So he and his team researched various assumptions about high-performing teams—team composition, "social competence, sensitivity training, various incentive systems, assessment centers, and outdoor wilderness teams." Their observations were always the same. They never found a direct correlation between these methods and the teams' actual performance (see_www.flowteam.com/e/2.htm). Gerber turned to complexity theory on the assumption that successful teams were self-organizing, an assumption that proved to be accurate. Gerber drew on his background in physics—as well as OD, training, and business—to develop FlowTeam Design, FlowStyleConference, and FlowStyleMeeting methodologies, which he applied in many businesses, including the global semi-conductor design and manufacturing organization where this example occurred.

FlowTeam Design (FlowTeam) has no actual relationship, according to Gerber, to the psychologically derived idea of *Flow* created by Mihaly Csikszentmihalyi and described in *The Psychology of Optimal Experience*. When participating in a FlowTeam, it nonetheless may feel much like what Csikszentmihalyi (1990) described: natural energizing processes engaged in pursuing an intrinsically meaningful goal that led to a creative zone of becoming one with the task. In Flow, the experience of time disappears.

FlowTeams engage learning that sits at the intersection of total chaos and predictable order. It is centered on achieving shared purpose, but to get there it invites exploration of new ways of thinking and goes beyond reliance on existing knowledge. FlowTeams rely on whole brain learning, sensory knowing, visualization, metaphor, and imagination. The process resembles Design Thinking's rapid prototyping, with a view to subsequent experimentation and evaluation. In doing so, participants stand on the edge of what they know individually and collectively. They pave new ground toward imagined, challenging states of new accomplishment.

FlowTeams are self-organizing and collectively self-directed. They begin with agreement on the team's shared purpose, as well as input into the process by which teams will work, identification of inputs and outputs, and understanding of resources that can be drawn upon to address the purpose.

The "soft" rules of FlowTeams support curiosity, brainstorming, and imagination through emphasis on "yes … and" (versus "no … but"), activating questions, active listening, reflection and "I" statements. Anyone can call "time out" when team members need to reflect or attend to group dynamics (e.g., integrate newcomers). Members call "time out" when they feel the group is stuck and wants input from other groups. Input is engaged through idea-generating Speed Presentations called by a particular team, or at suggested times, for sharing and thinking together. Each presenting group prepares a one-page, multi-sensory flipchart (or virtual display). When there are several Speed Presentations, they occur sequentially. They are short, about five minutes, and timed. Members sometimes walk around to give input into the initial phases of the process, or to refresh inputs or talk with someone from the group who elaborates on their thinking. Viewers post ideas, comments, suggestions, and questions on Post-it Notes (or virtual equivalents). The groups then go back to their teams, recharged by this infusion of others' perspectives. Members may also elect to join different teams if they are engaged by the other teams' topic. Thus, Flow is the ebb and flow of ideas, people, and energy—it's the movement that stimulates imagination.

Adopting and Adapting Flow

I encountered FlowTeams (Flow) when working with the Head of European Sales and an external consultant, Martin Gerber, who developed FlowTeam Design. Gerber was trained in physics. His speculation and analysis confirmed that high-performance teams exhibited the same phenomena as successful complex systems found in nature. He concluded that teams could be optimized by applying the basic operational principles of successful self-organizing complex systems—and translated them into 12 dynamics for people working in FlowTeams.[1]

The table stakes for Flow are defined right up front. You can't just throw a bunch of people together in a room and start a FlowTeam. Everybody in the room needs to understand the ultimate vision we're heading for, the outcomes we need. We need to agree that we really want to have as productive a team as possible; and we have to be clear on what our values are as a group or organization to keep the iterative process within those boundaries. If you can agree to those three things, then we can do Flow.

We met with the senior sales leaders in Rome. The senior leaders decided to employ a beginning FlowTeam session. They created high-level strategic desired outcomes, e.g., "We want to double revenues within three years, but maintain the headcount we have today with a stable cost structure." They liked Flow because it's very energizing. That planning stage took place before we gathered a much larger group for an Annual Learning Conference. We ended up with a FlowCongress—a modified FlowTeam Design. Rather than working on different challenges as is typically done, groups organized around the same focus. In this modified design, groups worked in different breakout rooms and moved back to the plenary room periodically for Speed Presentations. In FlowTeam Design, everyone usually works in the same large room so they can visit other groups freely, or engage in ad hoc speed presentations.

A bad financial quarter just before the Learning Conference led to another modification. We decided we could not fly all these people into one location and feed them for three days. The sales leader said, "Well, that's not a problem. Let's decide to meet in different cities (where the company is located). The three of us will travel as facilitators, or more accurately, activators. We'll keep the same input in each city group, but each country's output will be the input for the next one so they will build on what prior workshops produced."

So, we got everything together, divided up roles, and began the series of workshops, all of which took place in Europe. We followed FlowTeam Design as much as we possibly could. In the first city, in an open discussion (called meta generation), one of the groups said, "We started something that needs to be picked up, because we're not done with it, but it needs to be picked up by the next one. And what if that doesn't happen? No inflow."

In FlowTeams, you can't guarantee what the next group will choose to do. You provide the input, and it is left to the next group to decide if they want to pick this up. Even in a single FlowTeam session, there is no guarantee desired outputs from leadership will be picked up by teams. So participants in this first city's workshop proposed that each team that had an output they would like to be an input for the next city's workshop would send an ambassador to the next city's workshop. The ambassador could stay with a team adopting their input to work on it further or join another team, but they would still be an asset to working on the input they introduced if needed at any time in the process.

FlowTeam Dynamics

Gerber employed 12 Dynamics of FlowTeam Design. If he ran a workshop for 12 days, typically all 12 dynamics would show up; however, every group might not need to use all 12 dynamics. What was important was to let the process evolve naturally. When a team hit a rough spot or wasn't making progress, he would have them reflect and think about how they could solve that problem. He would say, "Okay, let's stop the action right here. Now, let's talk about what it is you're dealing with." For example, a person left your group because they had to go take a phone call, and they came back in and the group had to stop everything they were doing and spend up to 20 minutes getting them up to date. And this might keep happening. Gerber would say, "Well, that's a dynamic in a team that's working together that has to be dealt with. So how do you propose to work it?" And then they would make a flip chart. They would do a quick Flow one-pager to brainstorm the ways they could fix that.

Each team would capture dynamics they discovered and addressed them separately or as "input" to a consolidated group dynamics document, to guide them in the future and to continue to support the Flow process. For example, people might be frustrated with a person because they were moving to consensus and the outlier brought a different view that caused them to redo their conversation. But they also realized that the outcome was better. So they created a solution, e.g., naming what they saw happening, and they started to appreciate the outlier's contribution rather than getting annoyed with him or her. This dynamic is called "Genius Profiling," and generally occurs after teams have worked together over time. They have a little booklet now, which was how they kept team memory of pictures of flip charts and other team products. Members can still draw on this team memory when helpful.

The FlowTeam workshops were successful in achieving our goals. For five years, European sales wanted permission from headquarters to sell into the automotive industry. They were struggling with how to become virtually integrated with customers—by knowing what the customers needed and selling to these needs instead of what the factory makes. At that first meeting, one of the things people were most excited about was putting together information for a business plan for going into the automotive industry. Each city group identified information needed on the total available market in their region. So they would say to the next group, "Take this and run with it to add to the output." At the end of the fourth workshop, they had a one-page fact sheet that made the business case. U.S. senior management were convinced and it earned them entrée into the automotive industry.

Upsetting My Paradigm of L&D

FlowTeam Design upset my paradigm of learning design. L&D in the industrial era focused on subject-matter expertise. Just like the company was struggling to virtually integrate with customers, we had not thought about virtually integrating with learners. So a big shift for me was that we moved to learner-centric design. We had to know our learners way better than we knew them in the past, and we had to give them more control over what they needed and wanted to learn because what *I* think they need to learn is secondary to what *they* think they need to learn.

Engaging with FlowTeam Design showed Bill Gardner that L&D leaders need to rethink assumptions about high-quality learning under conditions of complexity. Decentering subject-matter experts validated everyone's experience and made space for listening to every voice. Using Post-it Notes engaged overlooked introverts. The environment maximized choice, purpose, and free-flowing conversation rather than control. The "fact sheet" generated new thinking that persuaded senior managers to change their strategy and sell into the automotive industry. Flow design opened the door to new ideas arising from the passion and vision of "edge players"— "people outside of traditional institutional boundaries" with "questioning dispositions … [that] lead them to discover and bring to the surface new practices and ultimately new institutional arrangements to support these dispositions" who "push the performance envelope" and work together to create new directions (Hagel III et al., 2010, p. 150). Generating multiple scenarios helped leaders in the organization expand the brief (Pendleton-Jullian & Brown, 2018a) and led to productive innovation.

Agile Team Experimentation and Learning

How can practices help organizations change the way they work in order to carry out new ideas? In the next vignette, we look at ways that larger, legacy industries are opening up to innovative, cross-boundary teaming. Sleeva (2021) shares her study of multiple agile teams focused on innovation in two leading organizations, one in healthcare and the other in insurance, that adapted agile practices in the technology function of their organizations. She illustrates the ways iterative experimentation helped teams learn by generating alternative ways of thinking and acting in the face of uncertainty. She also explores implications for boundary crossing and shared leadership.

BOX 7.3 AGILE INNOVATION—EXPERIMENTATION, BOUNDARY CROSSING, AND SHARED LEADERSHIP FOR TEAM LEARNING

Sheryl Sleeva, Ed.D., Head of New Ventures, Digital Network Services

The term "agile" is frequently applied to ways of working that are dynamic, nimble, customer-centric, and highly adaptive to change and uncertainty in complex organizational environments (Agile Alliance, 2022). The historical roots of agile date back to the "lean manufacturing" movement of the 1950s and 1960s, with its focus on productivity, continuous improvement, and customer value. However, its widespread adoption since the early 2000s is attributed to the success of agile methods in the software industry. The leading agile approach is Scrum, whose name is said to have been derived from the rugby term "scrummage" where teammates huddle to gain possession of the ball.

Agile approaches facilitate a team's ability to be nimble and "pivot" in order to adjust to change or respond to risk or uncertainty. Central is the use of small, self-organized, self-directed teams who develop customer-centered solutions in short multi-step work cycles called "sprints," where solution increments are iteratively developed, prototyped, and demoed. The cycle of sprints continues until the end product is delivered.

At the outset of agile development, the larger problem to be solved is carefully broken down by the team into smaller, workable increments (called "user stories"), so that each component can be rapidly developed, tested, and ultimately brought together into the larger whole following successive sprints. The facilitation of iterative experimentation and ability to incorporate ongoing customer feedback are core benefits of agile methods. They enable teams to co-create with customers, gain valuable real-time insights, quickly respond to changing requirements, and accelerate product delivery. Agile principles and practices support and facilitate team learning through creative problem solving, customer co-creation, perspective sharing, and thoughtful group reflection. Built into each cycle is dedicated time for critical reflection called the "agile retrospective," in which teams collectively learn from their experiences in the last sprint, making necessary adjustments to optimize successive development cycles. It is these characteristics, combined, that have enabled agile teams to achieve greater productivity and customer engagement than those using traditional development methods.

Software development is a team-driven innovation practice that is people intensive and has sizable costs and risks. Agile teams can achieve superior levels of productivity, while simultaneously developing and managing innovation work. By combining rapid execution with continuous innovation, agile practices help build organizational innovation capacity. Team learning is essential for innovation, and agile practices provide ongoing, immersive engagement in team problem solving, experimentation, and learning from experience.

Research Study

To explore innovation and team learning connections with agile practices, I conducted a multiple case study of software development teams that examined how agile teams learned and how they leveraged learning to innovate. Key findings centered around the wealth of informal and incidental team learning that occurs in agile innovation teams.

Iterative Experimentation

One of the most important ways agile practices foster team learning is through iterative experimentation. Experimentation optimizes learning through execution, enabling teams to effectively support customers, while innovating at the same time. Pendleton-Jullian & Brown (2018a) dedicated a chapter to the interplay of design thinking and learning with iterative experimentation:

> Rapid iteration in a problem solving setting … combines instrumental reasoning, or "figuring out what to do," with a tacit form of learning that takes place through action that is deeply embedded in the problem space … it transfers whole sets of interlinked skills and knowledge-building experience simultaneously. (p.68)

In my study, participants frequently cited how agile experimentation fostered innovation through test-driven development, prototyping, and customer co-creation. Team members shared that iterative experimentation sometimes meant "going down unhappy paths," but was perceived as critical to delivering solutions that improved the customer experience, while also building valuable team skills. Sometimes unsuccessful experiments in the short term proved to be fruitful in the longer term. One software engineer shared a story of the team euphoria that erupted when they achieved a key breakthrough after several frustrating sprints. However, this was quickly followed by disappointment when the solution was rejected by the customer during a subsequent demo session. The silver lining was that redemption occurred one year later when the team successfully deployed that very same solution for another important project, leveraging their learning to accelerate development time by several months. In software development where productivity is paramount, team learning outcomes like this can have significant bottom line and customer satisfaction impacts.

Another insight was how learning from iterative problem solving and experimentation is harvested through what is known as "failing fast." Study participants referenced this often, using similar phrases, also embraced in agile and lean methodology circles—such as, "failing better," "failing early," and "failing cheaply." One leader spoke about what failing fast meant to his team:

> I've always liked the "fail fast" mantra. If things work, great. If not, you take what you've learned and move on. If something doesn't work, you have to let it go. Not accepting that something didn't work out is a waste of time. You can't be afraid to try something. Just find out that it doesn't work quickly. (Sleeva, 2021, p. 135)

The philosophy of failing fast feels counterintuitive in many workplace cultures, where the pervasive view of failure is negative and is therefore to be avoided. As one participant stated, failing fast "doesn't always translate well in the organization regarding how people think about failure, risks, and trying new things." (Sleeva, 2021 p. 135). However, teams and organizations that are most successful implementing agile understand that failed experiments create prime opportunities to learn and innovate. As one participant put it, "The agile way is making many mistakes sooner and learning from those mistakes. When you're developing something in agile, you have to go through a lot of prototyping to get to something that really works" (Sleeva, 2021, p. 134).

Incremental development, testing, and learning from failure help agile teams to quickly identify what is not working, why, and whether a potential solution has value. This enables teams to experiment and problem solve, repeatedly and successfully. Smaller product increments and continual iteration with the customer each sprint cycle also help to "de-risk" development. Failing fast serves as both practical work strategy and cultural mindset, allowing teams to proactively pursue innovation, while remaining mindful of the associated costs and risks. By design, agile methods instill a time-bound discipline into each sprint that encourages teams to abandon less successful ideas in favor of alternative solutions. This prevents them from spiraling into a non-virtuous loop of experimentation in order to recoup sunk development costs.

Boundary Crossing and Shared Leadership

Other findings that support team learning included the cross-functional structure of agile teams. A typical agile team includes software developers, a product owner, and an agile process facilitator. In some organizations, individuals from other business functions (e.g., customer relationship management or finance) may also participate. Although not officially part of the agile team, customers (internal or external) closely collaborate throughout the process. These cross-functional, interdisciplinary, and cross-company interactions provide great opportunities for boundary crossing and facilitate team learning. Structurally speaking, agile teams are designed to be self-organizing, self-directed, and non-hierarchical. As such, leadership is typically shared among team members and individuals often report directly to managers outside of the team. While these self-directed agile teams have been found to be highly empowered, productive, and outcome-focused, traditional organizations that resist change can struggle to make these dimensions of agile implementation work, without major restructuring.

Scaling Agile

The study also showed that fully leveraging the benefits of agile innovation team learning requires scaling agile deployment, which for most organizations means undertaking the formidable endeavor of transformation. Implementing agile at scale presents significant challenges, most notably resistance to change—especially in large organizations where traditional development approaches and organizational structures predominate. The procedural and cultural shifts needed are complex, including the migration from hierarchical organization and management structures to highly empowered teams. For larger organizations, agile transformation is a disruptive, multi-year journey. Without the proper leadership support, employee buy-in, long-term focus, organizational courage, and persistence, the move to agile runs the risk of being unsuccessful.

Agile Philosophy and Guiding Principles

The use of agile practices continues to expand beyond the software industry into other strategic and organizational contexts. The original 2001 Agile Manifesto outlined a set of values and principles designed to transform the way that software development teams approached their work. These values and principles articulated what has become known as the "agile mindset," which is embraced by agile practitioners today. Other groups have endeavored to create manifestos of their own, including the Agile HR Manifesto, which was created by a group of 27 scholars and practitioners and has since garnered over 500 signatories (Almagro et al., 2017).

Agile in the Age of Digital Transformation

Agile methods are especially appealing in this digital age of accelerated change, complexity, globalization, risk, and uncertainty. By design, agile practices are flexible, adaptive, non-linear, customer-centric, and focused on continuous improvement, all of which work well in a VUCA world where continuous innovation has become table stakes. Practitioners of design thinking, lean, and agile continue to come together in exciting ways, for new product development, start-ups, platform innovation and industry transformation. Innovations embraced by one business function, industry, or sector can have a lot to offer others. As such, the road ahead for agile team learning in the age of digital transformation remains promising, as researchers and practitioners from multiple disciplines cross traditional boundaries and come together to collaborate, experiment, innovate, share, and learn.

LEARNING

Sleeva ends by addressing the challenges of scaling agile practices—centered in nimble, self-directed teams that by definition work across the otherwise siloed boundaries of the organization. Scaling can meet resistance in large, command-and-control, top-down organizations. The needs of innovation and the needs of standardized production may well be at odds with one another, and thus create challenges for drawing on agile in rethinking L&D in teams. Each organization needs to find answers to these dilemmas, to reap the benefits of team learning in the face of complexity and uncertainty. As Sleeva notes, however challenging, agile practices hold much promise for this fast-moving digital era that calls into question many of the assumptions of how work and learning are organized.

IMPLICATIONS FOR L&D

So why should L&D focus on team learning? Teams are the primary vehicle organizations use to roll out key development initiatives. They are the entry point for any development that goes beyond a focus on the individual. In these examples, we see the way in which teams are also a critical vehicle for learning. Understanding how teams learn, and particularly how they enable change and innovation in complexity, will enable L&D to better utilize teams to create the changes organizations need to survive and compete.

Tools and teaming structures can be offered as ways to experiment and learn. For example, Robbins' (2020) research showing that entrepreneurial teams fared better when using tools such as "turn taking, probing, and repair (error correction or gradual refinement—by self or other" (p. 15). Rules that become rigid are replaced by context-dependent guiding philosophies (agile) or principles (FlowTeams). Gerber, Flow's originator, identified 12 design dynamics that he waited to introduce until problems emerged that readied people for learning when the team was stuck. The design supported collective negotiation around a solution. Psychological safety (Edmondson, 2012, 2013) is evoked when caught up in a sea of group dynamics, power differentials, and norms representing differences in language, disciplinary, or functional expertise, or interpersonal conflicts.

Drawing on the Cynefin Framework (Snowden & Boone, 2007), as one moves from simple to complicated to complex decisions, rules dissolve and expected cause–effect formulae fail. Rethinking L&D for teams cannot be prescriptive, but developing a kit of practices and tools can help leaders and members engage in trial-and-trial as they act on boundaries, see how things change, and rethink and again reframe to experiment with a next round … and a next round … and a next round. All team members might not be ready to engage in these ways, but leaders need to cultivate environments and agreements that enable disrupting the status quo and learning one's way through. Further, as we note in the next chapter, a single leader acting alone cannot know enough to make such decisions. Knowledge resides in everyone, so shared decision making and learning are needed.

NOTE

1. www.flowteam.com/e/2.htm (accessed March 13, 2023).

8. Developing collective leadership—with Rachel Fichter

The true Master leads from behind, the people are hardly aware that he exists .... If you don't trust people, you make them untrustworthy. The Master speaks little .... He works without self-interest and leaves no trace. When the work is done, the people say: "Amazing: we did it, all by ourselves." Lao Tzu, Tao-te-ching, verse 17. 604 BC—To which we add: We did it collectively!

INTRODUCTION

In today's interconnected and technology-enabled world, when organizations take up leadership, they assume a tremendous responsibility, one that extends well beyond traditional organizational boundaries. They get pulled into a wide array of geopolitical emergencies (e.g., climate change, public health, social equity, wars). Leaders face unprecedented obstacles in balancing these conflicting priorities while simultaneously working to improve productivity and achieve increasingly aggressive performance goals. Leaders must learn to navigate their fast-changing business environments and also help the people "in their charge" (Sinek, 2019, p. 42) do the same. Learning and development (L&D) practitioners, in turn, must rethink leadership development to meet these new challenges.

In this chapter we explore how leadership development is evolving amidst complexity. The next section discusses the impact of complexity—specifically complex adaptive systems (CAS), dynamical systems, and bioecological perspectives—on organizations, given the interconnectedness of the world we live in. We argue that it is difficult, if not impossible, for any one individual to be the leader. A review of collective leadership literature then illustrates differences in interpretations and implications for practice. We discuss these next for L&D practitioners.

LEADING AMIDST COMPLEXITY

One way to make sense of how leadership development must change is to examine it through the lens of complexity. Complexity arises from problems "embedded within human contexts that organize themselves through changing social, political, economic, and cultural belief systems" (Pendleton-Jullian &

Brown, 2018a, p. 45). Organizations are part of CASs, which "are found in the transitional space between order and chaos" (Pendleton-Jullian & Brown, 2018a, p. 45) whose members modify "the system through their interaction with it, and with each other" (p. 47).

Coleman et al. (2017) offer a related perspective on complexity in organizations as "dynamical systems composed of sets of interconnected elements … that change and evolve over time as they interact with each other" (p. 182). As mutually influencing elements interact, they contribute to the evolution of the system over time. But the system does not end at the boundaries of the organization.

Leaders are at the fulcrum of these complex, co-evolving systems. In addition to managing the day-to-day operations of a business and taking care of the people in their charge, they are also increasingly responsible for driving innovation and culture change. However, in a CAS world, that means consciously negotiating with and influencing the environment, acting as purposeful "micro-modulators … that do work within the system, altering the system and its evolution" (Pendleton-Jullian & Brown, 2018a, p. 48). Instead of trying to address individual problems as they arise, micro-modulators tackle the context within which a problem manifests. This requires an ability to understand all aspects of the context and how they affect the problem (and, to underscore the interdependence of CAS, how the problem also affects the context). Complexity research has pointed to the importance of diverse networks to solve problems, foster innovation, and enact change in complex environments. For instance, Hagel III et al. (2010) describe the intentional creation of "weak ties" to build "rich networks of relationships" (p. 15) that shape serendipitous encounters to support learning and innovation. Similarly, Rogers et al. (2005) coined the term "cosmopolites" to characterize "locally networked system members with heterogeneous weak ties to outside systems" (p. 4) as a means to forge the connections necessary to understand context and exert more control over outcomes. These networks of interdependent relationships create a web of influence (Wheatley, 2011) that is more powerful than a lone individual leader. Wheatley and Frieze (2006) note:

> But networks aren't the whole story. As networks grow and transform into active, working communities of practice, we discover how life truly changes, which is through emergence. When separate, local efforts connect with each other as networks, then strengthen as communities of practice, suddenly and surprisingly a new system emerges at a greater level of scale. This system of influence possesses qualities and capacities that were unknown in the individuals. It isn't that they were hidden; they simply don't exist until the system emerges. They are properties of the system, not the individual, but once there, individuals possess and can exercise them. And the system that emerges always possesses greater power and influence

than is possible through planned, incremental change. Emergence is how life creates radical change and takes things to scale. (p. 148)

Leadership in this context is necessarily more collaborative.

COLLECTIVE LEADERSHIP

No longer able to rely on traditional hierarchical leadership structures that emphasize the authority of the individual leader, some organizations are beginning to look to processes of collective leadership for complex problem solving (e.g., Croft et al., 2022; Eva et al., 2021; Ospina, 2020). Collective leadership—characterized variously as shared, distributed, plural, or inclusive—is contextual and amorphous. Broadly, it is a "fluid and dynamic process around the granting and claiming of leadership roles" (Eva et al., 2021, p. 1) in which individuals enter and exit those roles "over time in both formal and informal relationships" (Yammarino et al., 2012, p. 382). Embedded in that definition is the notion that leadership is no longer a defined position tied to a single person, but a "set of behaviors … with different team members assuming the mantle of leader as required by situational factors" (Eva et al., 2021, p. 1). Similarly, Raelin (2016) conceptualizes "Leadership-as-Practice" (L-A-P) as "intrinsically collective" (p. 4) and "occurring as a practice rather than residing in the traits or behaviors of particular individuals" (p. 1). No longer dependent on an assumption of followership, L-A-P "depicts immanent collective action emerging from mutual, discursive, sometimes recurring and sometimes evolving patterns in the moment and over time among those engaged in the practice" (p. 3) resulting from day-to-day experiences.

Croft et al. (2022) distinguish between collective work, "characterized by alignment and coordination of activities in contexts where individuals still pursue their own divergent aims," and collective leadership, as "the interaction of strategic ambiguity and inward- and outward- facing reification practices to maintain divergent perspectives alongside agreed collective aims, alignment and coordination of activities, and commitment to collective success" (p. 483). This viewpoint is redolent of the Center for Creative Leadership's Direction, Alignment, Commitment (DAC) model in which all three elements must be present for leadership to be effective (Center for Creative Leadership, 2020). In the context of collective leadership, this means that the collective's membership must set their direction (i.e., it cannot be defined by anyone outside the group), align and coordinate work, and demonstrate commitment to the group and its direction.

In a comprehensive literature review, Eva at al. (2021) identified five perspectives on collective leadership: person-centric, social network, socio-relational, sociomaterial, and institutional. Informed by theories of leadership as an individual endeavor, the person-centric approach "emerges at the crossroads of a distribution of the leadership role, diverse skills and expertise within the network, and the effective exchange of information among team members in order to capitalize on and coordinate their role behaviors and expertise" (Friedrich, 2009, p. 935). While still predominantly individual in nature, the social network view acknowledges the interpersonal nature of leadership as a "dyadic, shared, relational, strategic, global, and a complex social dynamic" (Avolio et al., 2009, p. 423) and is characterized by the extent of ties to others in the system. By contrast, the socio-relational perspective represents a significant shift away from "great man" theories of leadership with social relationships as "both the core unit of analysis and the basis for leadership emergence and development processes" (Eva et al., 2021, pp. 3–4). The sociomaterial lens incorporates the relational aspect of leadership but also sees leadership "as a configuration of social, material and discursive relations (e.g., connections, practices and routines) in everyday management work" (Eva et al., 2021, p. 4). Reflecting the sociomaterial approach, Raelin's (2016) L-A-P describes leadership as "embodied through language and through other semiotic manifestations in conjunction with the material, structural, and aesthetic resources within the actual workings of practice rather than through individual a priori intentions" (p. 5). Finally, the institutional view explores the tension between an organization's past, present, and future, especially through discourse on core values as a way of encouraging organizational transformation.

Collective leadership does not, however, stop at organizational boundaries. Building on the earlier discussion of complexity, a sixth perspective advocates for leadership collectives, or "groups of individuals from multiple organisations and sectors who lead transformational social change together through critical reflection, inclusivity and care" (Care et al., 2021). Indeed, collective leadership can be particularly powerful for the most complex and entrenched problems, because it is only through the collective that it is possible to strategically and intentionally evolve the system. In the vignette that follows, we see how the DAO enacts collective leadership.

BOX 8.1 THE DAO

Rachel Fichter, Adjunct Faculty, Teachers College, Columbia University

One form of collective leadership that aligns to the sociomaterial perspective is the decentralized autonomous organization (DAO). A digital organization construct characterized by the interaction between people (socio) and technology (material), the DAO allows people to collaborate on shared goals without a traditional management hierarchy. The first DAO was built in 2015 (Santana & Albareda, 2022) on Ethereum, a blockchain "technology for building apps and organizations, holding assets, transacting and communicating without being controlled by a central authority" (Ethereum.org, 2022, para. 2). Since then, DAOs have begun to proliferate. According to the DAO analytics site DeepDAO, as of September 18, 2022 there were 4,830 DAOs with almost 5 million participants.

The DAO "lives on the internet and exists autonomously, but also heavily relies on hiring individuals to perform certain tasks that the automaton itself cannot do" (Buterin, 2014, para. 14). A central component of the DAO is the smart contract, which holds the treasury and the rules that underpin decision making: "Once the contract is live on Ethereum .... If anyone tries to do something that's not covered by the rules and logic in the code, it will fail" (Ethereum.org, 2022, para. 3). Effective governance is achieved through a combination of on-chain and off-chain processes. *On-chain* refers to processes that happen directly on the platform according to rules specified in the blockchain programming code. *Off-chain* governance involves all formal and informal governance-related decisions, including establishing and evolving the parameters for the DAO's smart contract. Off-chain governance discussions typically take place on social media, in online forums, and at conferences. While the smart contract is fundamental to the structure of the DAO, there are no set guidelines for off-chain governance. DAOs typically take an iterative approach to determining how decisions will be made, updating their bylaws as they learn from their experiences.

One example of a DAO experimenting with alternative forms of decision making to produce large-scale change is the Optimism Collective. Established by Optimism Public Benefit Corporation (PBC) (recently split into two entities: OP Labs PBC and the Optimism Foundation), the company behind a blockchain technology designed to improve the scale and speed of Ethereum transactions, the Optimism Collective's vision is to "sustainably fund those public goods that improve upon the well-being of the Collective and beyond" (Optimism, 2022a, para. 1). Unlike traditional corporations, which often have a charitable-giving arm but are primarily focused on generating profits for shareholders, all revenues from the Optimism blockchain go to the Optimism Collective for the purpose of retroactive public goods funding (i.e., rewarding projects that have already delivered value) because "it's easier to agree on what was useful than what will be useful" (Buterin, 2021a, para. 6). Ultimately, the Optimism Collective has little to do with blockchains; its primary objective is to fund initiatives that are important for society to thrive but have not been adequately funded. Over time, the Collective aims to become a fully functioning—albeit digital—organizing system that will support a range of projects, from internet technologies to education and the arts.

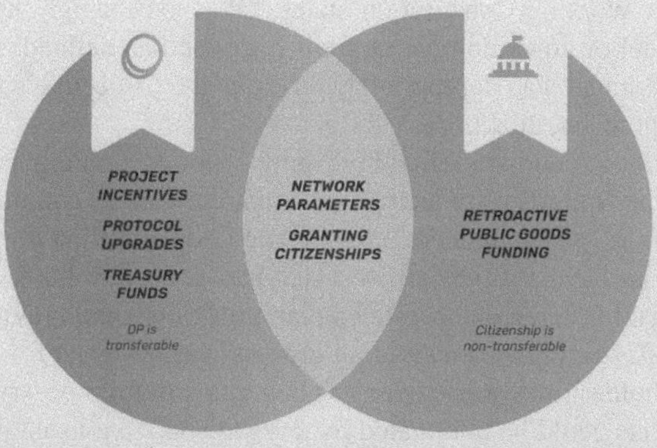

Source: https://optimism.mirror.xyz/gQWKlrDqHzdKPsB1iUnI-cVN3v0NvsWnazK7ajlt1fI

Figure 8.1.1 The Optimism Collective's governance structure

The Optimism Collective is governed by the Token House and the Citizens' House, two off-chain structures. Comprising Optimism (OP) token holders, Token House members are tasked with making decisions mainly related to capital allocation. Certain votes need simple majorities (51%); others require super majorities (76%). A period of reflection follows each decision-making session, with improvements documented in the OPerating (*sic*) Manual (Ethereum-Optimism, n.d.) and maintained on GitHub for transparency. The Token House is a liquid democracy, a democratic system that uses both direct and representative voting. Token House members may delegate their voting power to someone who has the domain knowledge necessary to make an informed decision. However, unlike in a traditional representative democracy with election cycles, token holders can revoke their support for a representative at any time.

Based on the belief that token holders are more incentivized to make decisions that will increase the value of the OP token in the short term, Optimism established the Citizens' House to ensure the long-term sustainability of the system and achieve its long-term vision. Members of the Citizens' House, themselves beneficiaries of the Collective, are responsible for distributing retroactive public goods funding. According to one community member: "When we [the Optimism Collective] think of ourselves as an organizing system, the people who we are trying to sustain are our citizens. We need to give the people who would be getting grants a voice."

The Collective see its governance as an "experiment" that will "evolve with community participation, growth, and learning" (Optimism, 2022a, para. 1). With an initial lifespan of "no more than four years," the

Collective's Working Constitution states, "It is exceedingly unlikely that a fixed model of governing the Optimism Collective, defined at the outset of this experiment, can appropriately navigate the Collective's future challenges" (Optimism, 2022b, para. 2).

In an initial round of retroactive public goods funding just prior to launching the Optimism Collective, Optimism invited 22 community members (known as "badge holders") to allocate USD 1 million in profits from the Optimism blockchain to projects that had delivered more value to the Optimism and Ethereum ecosystems than profit they had previously made (Buterin, 2021b). Optimism's voting process was designed for transparency: badge-holder rules were given explicit and carefully observed instructions; projects could be nominated by anyone and were listed publicly; all badge-holder discussions took place in public forums; and the final results, including individual badge-holder votes, were publicly announced.

Several key learnings emerged during a post-vote reflection period, most notably that, "due to some combination of choice of badge holders and subconscious biases" (Buterin, 2021b, para. 5), every winner was a technology project even though there was nothing in the instructions specifying project type. This led to the establishment of several project categories and committees with domain expertise for each category. Another outcome of the first funding round was the recognition that this type of process could not be executed by OP token holders who are more focused on short-term incentives than on long-term vision, which resulted in the addition of the Citizens' House to the Collective's governance.

As this vignette illustrates, leadership by an organizational collective is possible, and it requires clear and transparent guidelines. Processes for equitable decisions are used to lessen undue influence of biases and power dynamics.

COLLECTIVE LEADERSHIP DEVELOPMENT

If the definitional "plasticity" (Croft et al., 2022) of collective leadership makes it difficult to pinpoint exactly what collective leadership is, any discussion of how to develop it is likely to involve experimentation. A useful starting point is to establish some clarity by distinguishing collective leadership from leader and leadership development. Leader development (often incorrectly framed as leadership development) focuses on enhancing the knowledge and skills of the individual leader (Eva et al., 2021; Raelin, 2016) based on a competency or capability framework aligned to an organization's strategic goals. Often taking a one-size-fits-all approach, interventions of this type emphasize the development of "normative" (Eva et al., 2021) behaviors (i.e., those designed to meet a certain standard). These programs tend to produce leaders who are consumed "by the idea that they must be inspiring, visionary, connected to people in transformational relationships, more emotionally intelligent, and so on, rather than being equipped to deal with complex, collaborative, cross-boundary, adaptive work in which they are increasingly engaged" (Denyer & James, 2016, p. 263) and act "in isolation to others and context" (p. 263). Also, often normative (even if otherwise stated), leadership development is a "process … that inherently involves multiple individuals (e.g., leaders and followers or among peers in a self-managed work team)" (Day et al., 2014, p. 64). Leadership development is also "inherently multilevel and longitudinal" (p. 64) because of how it "involves mapping and understanding within- and between-person change patterns—as well as those involving groups, teams, and larger collectives—over time …. This longitudinal, multilevel focus means that intrapersonal and interpersonal processes are central to leadership development over time" (p. 64).

By contrast, collective leadership development—in particular the socio-material perspective—is "critical" (Day et al., 2014, p. 64) with the intention of disrupting existing norms and challenging the status quo. It is highly contextual to the collective and the system within which it operates.

Definitions of collective leadership (Table 8.1) have several shared assumptions that can provide the basis for a meaningful exploration of how it is developed.

Collective leadership is,

1. a *process* that evolves through dialogue among its members;
2. an *outcome* that is the result of effective dialogue among its members;
3. distributed across a *network* of people who come together to define and achieve a goal;
4. determined by *context* and the specific situation to be addressed or goal to be achieved;
5. *diverse* to reflect the unique skills, perspectives, and experiences of each member;
6. *dynamic* in terms of membership to meet the needs of the situation; and
7. *non-hierarchical* where no individual can veto the decisions of the collective.

One example of collective leadership development builds on action learning and coaching. Leadership in International Management (LIM) develops shared leadership disciplines based on five Cs: connect, contract, collect, collaborate, and challenge.[1] What follows is a discussion of possible developmental supports that reinforce the assumptions outlined above and can, when woven together, create a holistic collective leadership development experience that supports short-term organizational performance and long-term collective growth.

Table 8.1 Collective leadership definitions and assumptions

Source	Definition	Assumptions	Developmental Supports
Friedrich et al., 2009	"a dynamic leadership process in which a defined leader, or set of leaders, selectively utilize skills and expertise within a network, effectively distributing elements of the leadership role as the situation or problem at hand requires" (p. 933)	Process, context, networks, dynamic, diverse	Organizational Network Analysis (ONA); Systemic Coaching; Action Learning
Yammarino et al., 2012	"multiple individuals assuming (and perhaps divesting themselves) of leadership roles over time in both formal and informal relationships" (p. 382)	Context, dynamic, diverse	ONA; Systemic Coaching
Gram-Hanssen, 2021	"leadership in processes of transformational community change … is inherently collective and emergent while simultaneously being dependent on individuals … contributing … their unique skills and perspectives toward the greater good" (p. 536)	Process, outcome, diverse, context (goal)	Dialogic OD; Dialogic Scenarios (and conversational choice-points); Collaborative Leadership Learning Groups (CLLGs)
Croft et al., 2022	"the interaction of strategic ambiguity and reification practices to maintain divergent perspectives alongside agreed collective aims, alignment and coordination of activities, and commitment to collective success" (p. 483)	Process, outcome, diverse, context (goal)	Dialogic OD; Action Learning; CLLGs
Raelin, 2016	"leadership as a social, material, and jointly accomplished process" (p. 1)	Process, networks, diverse, context (goal)	Dialogic OD; Dialogic Scenarios (and conversational choice-points); ONA; Action Learning; CLLGs; Systemic Coaching

Source: Rachel Fichter.

Dialogic Organization Development (OD)

Foundational to collective leadership development and all seven assumptions identified above is the importance of effective dialogue, with an emphasis on listening and reflection:

> The parties to the practice engage in semiotic, often dialogical, exchange, and in some cases for those genuinely committed to one another, they display an interest in listening to one another, in reflecting on new perspectives, and in entertaining the prospect of changing direction based on what they learn. (Raelin, 2016, p. 4)

One way to build skillful engagement is Dialogic Organization Development (OD) (Eva et al., 2021). Unlike Diagnostic OD, in which practitioners typically collect and analyze data to make a "diagnosis" against a predetermined future state as the basis for organizational transformation, Dialogic OD is based on the premise that transformation is inherently emergent and happens organically through changes in organizational narratives. Thus, the aim of Dialogic OD is to foster "generativity to develop new possibilities rather than problem-solving, altering the prevailing narratives and stories that limit new thinking, and working with the self-organizing, emergent properties of complex systems" (Bushe & Marshak, 2016, p. 407). Dialogic OD is rooted in eight dialogic mindsets (pp. 409–410):

1. reality and relationships are socially constructed;
2. organizations are meaning-making systems;
3. language, broadly defined, matters;
4. creating change requires changing conversations;
5. groups and organizations are inherently self-organizing;
6. differentiation in participative inquiry and engagement should be increased before seeking coherence;
7. transformational change is more emergent than planned;
8. consultants are a part of the process, not apart from the process.

Dialogic OD is particularly suited to collective leadership development because it sees the collective as a powerful source of change when complexity makes certainty of the outcome impossible. An organization achieves its change goals not by prescribing them but by inviting the collective to explore how to alter everyday conversations in ways that open up new possibilities for growth and success. Dialogic OD is inclusive and generative; it invites those who question convention and challenge the status quo to share their perspectives and broaden the experience of the collective.

Bushe and Marshak (2016) identify 40 forms of Dialogic OD, some of them structured (i.e., events or experiences orchestrated by a practitioner to create a container for generative conversations) and others unstructured (i.e., situations in which the practitioner brings a "dialogic mindset" to help "individuals become aware of and take more control over the prevailing images, metaphors, and narratives that are shaping how people think and act" (p. 3)). Examples of structured events include World Café, Open Space Technology, Six Conversations, Social Labs, and Appreciative Inquiry (AI).

Dialogic Scenarios

A second dialogue-based method for developing collective leadership is Dialogic Scenarios, an exploration of common patterns of conversation that unfold over time (Gergen & Hersted, 2016). While these scenarios are so ingrained that they often "seem biological in origin" (p. 183), they are the result of social constructions and can be consciously reshaped by the collective to produce change. Three types of dialogic scenarios—sustaining, generative, and degenerative—are most critical for skilled dialogue. Sustaining dialogues are "water cooler" types of conversations without specific business goals that serve to establish trust and strengthen relationships. In generative dialogues, participants listen deeply to one another and, by building on each other's contributions, engage in "learning, creativity, and possibly a sense of delight" (p. 183) to achieve a collective goal. By contrast, degenerative scenarios are about "silence, animosity, or the breaking of a relationship altogether. They may begin subtly: one offers a proposal, and the reply is a critique; one gives an order, and there is sullen resistance; one blames the other, and the reply is counter-blame. All these adjacency pairs can invite subsequent degeneration" (Gergen & Hersted, 2016, p. 183).

To help the collective learn to transform degenerative dialogues into generative ones, practitioners might suggest role-play and reflection, asking questions like, "How would you characterize the scenario in this conversation?" (p. 189). Next, using "conversational choice-points" (Gergen & Hersted, 2016, p. 183), the collective considers how it might alter the role-play conversation to make it less antagonistic and then practices those changes to strengthen its skills in generative dialogue.

Action Learning

Action learning (AL) is one of several dialogue-based interventions known as "action modalities" (Raelin, 2016, p. 7) in which people work together and reflect on their experience to build their overall problem-solving capacities (Raelin, 2016). A form of work-based learning, action learning "uses work on an actual project or problem as the way to learn. Participants work in small groups to take action to solve their problem and learn how to learn from that action" (O'Neil & Marsick, 2007, p. xvii). A core premise of AL is that learning can be facilitated through questions and dialogue, which help participants see different perspectives as they work together on a problem. AL develops *questioners* rather than *question-answerers*, organic risk takers rather than functional experts, and leaders rather than specialists. The form of AL most relevant to collective leadership development is rooted in the critical reflection school of thought, which focuses on individual and organizational transformation by challenging existing ways of thinking and working. AL is often supported by a coach who "leads reflection and helps participants uncover, challenge, and change assumptions about the organization and themselves that shape their views and actions" (Faller et al., 2020, p. 293). The critical, contextual, and experimental aspects of action learning make it particularly relevant for developing collective leadership (Eva at al., 2021).

The critical forms of action learning disrupt reliance on old mindsets, practices, and leadership cultures that need transformation. In the following vignette, AL is paired with Dialogic OD (Box 8.2). Corrie et al. (2020) sought to transform the diagnostic culture of the National Health Service and Army Medical Service using narrative and dialogic coaching. In a two-part, three-day workshop, each leader shared a disorienting leadership dilemma and then retold their story as critical self-examination. During a month's break, participants were then asked to: (1) write a short narrative professional analysis of what happened; (2) "subjectively explore alternative perspectives … of a selected other" in the story; and (3) expand their story "using an artistic medium of their choice." They shared these "creative artefacts" in the next session. They then "again used action learning and group coaching to reflect on and challenge assumptions around their personal, professional, and organisational transformation" (Corrie et al., 2020, p. 44). The physiotherapy team lead, for example, shared insight into collective team leadership in the form a large colorful 3D hand with numerous, overlapping, multi-colored hands covering the surface:

> I was very taken by the stories on day one from the army and I've written my own (… personal story of challenge trauma and learning in which the key thread was that of helping each other with resilience) …. I need to embrace "the difference" in others and see things from their perspective and remind myself that leaders and managers are part of the team too. (Corrie et al., 2020, p. 47)

In Box 8.2, Corrie describes the disruptive pedagogy that he and other facilitators designed. Action Learning Conversations—a stand-alone, structured protocol that Marsick and O'Neil (2009) developed using questioning, assumption-identification, and reframing—were used to further deepen access to taken-for-granted assumptions, values, and beliefs that artifacts revealed.

BOX 8.2 TRANSFORMING LEADERSHIP IN THE UK DEFENCE MEDICAL SERVICES

Dr Ian Corrie, Associate Professor, Leadership and Innovation, University of Cumbria, UK.

In collaboration with Brigadier Toby Rowland, Defence Medical Services, UK

In response to a UK government report detailing systemic failures in the National Health System (NHS), I was asked as a member of the university teaching faculty to develop a new leadership program for an NHS hospital. With the goal of transforming the culture from one of transactional to something more caring and inclusive, I drew from transformative learning and action learning theories to develop a *disruptive pedagogy* intended to challenge the assumptions, values, and beliefs that had shaped the culture into what it was and laid the foundation for positive culture change. After delivering and evaluating the pilot we applied this to the military medical environment.

For the participants, the disruptions were not only cognitive; they were also material. Participants expected PowerPoints, traditional leadership theory, and didactic teaching: "Tell me what I need to write and what I need to know." We removed all of that. We offered a leadership program with no leadership theory in it whatsoever, because it was all about them as leaders (people). So, they experienced a disorienting dilemma from the very beginning. We started by undertaking critical reflection with them. That surprised them. And then there was the unexpected request to examine their own experience in their leadership roles rather than passively listen to lectures on leadership. This also surprised them.

We also carefully considered how to create the ideal environment for learning. Then we examined who was running the program. Instead of being their "teacher," I played the role of "facilitator," as a coach, removing the traditional power dynamics to focus on the participants as the most important people in the room. They knew what they needed to do. They just needed me to guide them rather than put barriers up as the "professor." We didn't allow any insignias, they didn't wear uniforms, the overt power was removed, we took them out of their comfortable context. One of the most important parts about this approach is how you create the ideal environment for facilitation. My experience is that if you don't get that right, you won't get the same impact. In a sense, our relationship with them created the ideal environment for their relationship with themselves. It allowed them to open up to self-dialogue.

The three main elements of the new program—transformative leadership, coaching, and action learning—were underpinned by critical self-reflection (see Figure 8.2.1 below). In order to elicit a change in oneself, one first has to become aware of the values and beliefs that underlie behavior. So first, we examined the values. We then examined the beliefs that underpinned those values, and we got them to reflect on what impact it had on their team and organization. We also used the framework for them to reflect on their authenticity as leaders, checking espoused perspective of self, versus reality. We asked them to pick a work situation and used a perspective positioning exercise to get them to see the situation first from their own point of view, the others, and then as a "fly on the wall." This enabled them to consider how their behavior might be viewed by others. Then we got them to reflect by asking, "So what now? How might you have dealt with the situation differently?"

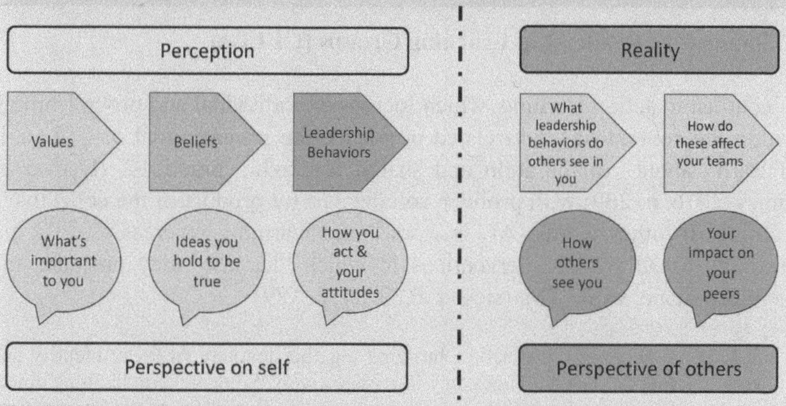

Source: Author.

Figure 8.2.1 Values, beliefs, behaviors model: perception versus reality

To encourage deeper reflection, we invited participants to create an artifact as a manifestation of their learning journey. Later they shared their artifacts with each other and provided critique and support. It was an opportunity to become more vulnerable. After that, they tended to open up more to each other as a team.

In addition to using action learning with leadership program participants to help them learn how to learn to solve problems more effectively, we organized action learning sets for special interest groups from across the different defense medical healthcare areas. The learning sets became small communities of professional practice within the broader group, which was a bigger community of professional practice. At each stage we asked, "What was a key takeaway for you?" and "What would you now do differently?" Some of the takeaways about personal life were quite deep.

Perspective positioning did open participants to different viewpoints and enable them as leaders to better support, mentor, and develop others as leaders. They became more aware of others' perspectives. One senior leader, when asked if the program had an impact, replied, "I have long felt a victim of the consequence of cultures and behaviors often exhibited by (other professional groups) resulting in the assumption that there was nothing to be done than to accept my position in the hierarchy. ... My perspective has been softened to make allowances for values, beliefs and behaviors of others (medical doctors) and to understand how I might best use my new insight to challenge these maladaptive frames of reference in self and others."

Collaborative Leadership Learning Groups (CLLGs)

In contrast to action learning, which focuses on individual and group learning within the context of work-related problems, the primary goal of CLLGs is to learn "about collaboration and shared leadership practices" (Denyer & James, 2016, p. 269) with problem solving as a by-product of the collective's learning. In other words, AL is work-based learning, whereas CLLGs are "learning-based work" interventions in which "learning may precede, and therefore shape, work" (Marsick et al., 2021, p. 179).

> CLLGs are anchored in practice, bringing together learners who can identify and work together on the challenges they face collectively. Some general learning objectives for the program may be described to help scope and focus the intervention, but the precise learning outcomes cannot be predetermined because learners decide collectively on what they hope to accomplish to achieve their mission. (Denyer & James, 2016, p. 269)

CLLGs are grounded in three sources of knowing: (1) knowledge and experiences brought by the learners; (2) publicly available practical and theoretical knowledge; and (3) knowledge created by the collective as the result of its interactions. Instead of a facilitator, CLLGs have an "orchestrator" responsible for creating a safe space for participants to "explore the tensions, difficult experiences, and emotions involved in leadership" (Denyer & James, 2016, p. 269).

Systemic Coaching

Intended to trigger experimentation within the L&D practitioner community, the tools and frameworks outlined above are just a few of many ways to develop collective leadership, but they all assume that individual leaders are ready to participate in a collective. Becoming a collective leader implies thinking interdependently and relationally because change occurs through the relationships among many interconnected pieces. Solving complex problems depends on the capacity to put in relationship many different perspectives and sets of expertise. However, getting to this awareness is not always easy. For example, leaders can be embedded in rigid or bureaucratic structures or mindsets, or challenged when venturing beyond their functional area where their expertise is understood and valued.

Systemic coaching in one-way organizations can help their members see the value of interdependence and connect what they do with other parts in the system (Clutterbuck, 2007; Hawkins & Turner, 2020; Lawrence, 2019). Systemic coaching develops recognition that learning and development grows through relationships between an organism or living system and the wider living ecosystems in which it is embedded. Clutterbuck (2007) contrasts "thinking systematically" with "thinking systemically." It is a way of thinking that helps coach and coachee avoid engaging in over-simplistic analyses, and coming up with over-simplistic solutions because the coach helps the coachee explore, learn, and develop in relation to the worlds they are embedded within (Hawkins & Turner, 2020). A systemic approach to coaching can be used both in individual and team coaching as illustrated by the LeadPharma program (Box 8.3).

BOX 8.3 SYSTEMIC COACHING

Pierre Faller, Ed.D., Lecturer, Teachers College, Columbia University

"LeadPharma" is a leadership development program for high potential leaders in a large pharmaceutical company. The program is a six-month intense learning experience, blending in-person lectures, online webinars, and individual coaching. Over the course of the program, participants meet with their coach six times for one-hour coaching conversations. Coaches hired for the program all have experience in systemic coaching. Two critical developmental areas leaders are invited to explore are enterprise mindset and change agility. *Enterprise mindset* means to develop the capacity to think broader, see the bigger picture, take the larger organization into account when making decisions and setting priorities. *Change agility* is a broader capacity to think ahead, navigate ambiguity, or flexibly pivot when conditions evolve. In each case, there is a need to increase awareness of the whole system and the different complex parts that interact within it.

Coaches help participants develop a broad understanding of their ecosystem and the challenges they face in connection to the whole system. To do that, coaches invite their clients to rethink their role and goals by taking a "stakeholder" perspective. One tool that is frequently used is DeLuca's (1999) organizational map model. The map requires clients to think about questions such as: (1) Who are the key players? (2) What is their power/influence in the organization? (3) To what extent are they applying their influence for or against the issue? (4) How easily can their applied influence be changed? (5) What significant relationships exist among the key players? Often, coaches also conduct 30-minute conversations with key stakeholders to provide the client with different views and perspectives on their work. Later on, clients are invited to bring their maps into action and develop a concrete plan identifying specific goals, actions, and timing for each important stakeholder. This plan is then shared and discussed with the coachee's manager and skip-level manager, who share ideas about the ways they can support the coachee as he or she continues to develop important relationships across the organization.

In an example of systemic team coaching, TopHealth is a leadership development program taking place in a large healthcare system. The largest component of the program is Action Learning (AL), a coach-facilitated experiential platform where people work in small teams to identify solutions to complex organizational problems. In TopHealth, physician leaders develop a broad systemic view by teaming with other physician leaders who work in different areas. Over five months, they meet regularly to collaboratively explore an important question about the organization's future, for which there is no obvious solution and more learning is needed. Some questions teams have explored in the past include how to create better communication systems among physicians, align incentives across the system, enhance innovation for clinical excellence.

AL coaches meet with their team once a month for half a day. The coach helps the team recognize the underlying complexity of the question they are asked to explore and learn more before examining possible options. The emphasis therefore is on problem framing rather than problem solving. Through dialogic and reflective spaces, coaches help team members step back, share, examine and challenge different assumptions about what the problem might be. AL coaches also invite team members to test their assumptions by collecting information across the organization. They are encouraged to meet with internal stakeholders and gather as many organizational perspectives as possible. This phase often leads teams to revisit their initial assumptions and reframe their understanding of the problem. At the end of the program, each team is invited to present their exploration and recommendations to ten senior administrators (including CEO and COO), who are invited to react, question and dialogue with the teams.

CONCLUSIONS

Table 8.2 *Collective leadership shift in L&D focus*

From	To
Individual leader development	Group leadership development
Self-awareness	Self-as-part-of-systems awareness
Competency development	Conversation development
Change management – prescriptive	Change emergence – generative
Separated	Networked
Diagnostic	Dialogic

Source: Rachel Fichter.

L&D professionals can influence a shift toward collective leadership in organizations by designing for the seven assumptions of collective leadership identified earlier in relationship to Table 8.1.

A first step is to define group leadership development goals, in addition to individual ones, when planning leadership programs. One such goal is to foster generativity by building group conversation capabilities instead of individual leadership competencies. Next, there is an opportunity to add a systems lens to self-awareness by incorporating systemic individual coaching to prepare a leader for participation in collective leadership, and systemic team coaching to enhance the collective's capacities for driving complex change. For the L&D practitioner this means adopting a dialogic OD mindset and getting comfortable with the idea that change in any complex system cannot be managed or prescribed; rather, it emerges through intentional conversation and conscious participation in the evolution of a system. While these approaches may create challenges for fledgling collectives operating in traditional organizations (and for the L&D practitioners supporting them), the potential for enacting positive, sustainable change amidst complexity is tremendous.

NOTE

1. Video description—https://www.limglobal.net/ (accessed March 12, 2023).

9. Rethinking evaluation of L&D

Some leaders believe they do not need to measure learning; they can observe it in their subordinate's behavior. But others question the value human resource development (HRD) adds to the organization. Is learning and development (L&D) measuring what organizations actually value? Learning analytics now permit precise measurement of many aspects of learning in the workplace, but what should we measure to know if we are actually contributing to enhancing individual capacity and that of the organization? This chapter looks at current advances using Artificial Intelligence (AI), nudging technologies, and other means to deepen L&D's capacity to measure impact. The use of qualitative approaches to capture learning in the workplace is also discussed.

ASKING THE RIGHT QUESTIONS

Early evaluation models focused on Kirkpatrick's four levels of evaluation—reaction, learning, behavior, and results (Kirkpatrick, 1983)—and on return on investment, which Phillips (1998) argued is the fifth level of evaluation. Kirkpatrick's levels of evaluation are not actually levels but rather different types of variables that should be measured to determine the effectiveness of learning and development. At the reaction level, we look at learner satisfaction with a learning event or program. Learning looks at what was learned—the knowledge, skills, and attitudes attained. Behavior measures whether or not the learner's behavior actually changed—are they using the new skills on the job? Results are interpreted broadly—with some looking at Return on Investment (ROI) at this point, although the original intent was to suggest that developers needed to explore whether or not the learning or training conducted actually addressed the organizational need that led to its being offered and that that learning transferred to the workplace. Since this learning occurs in the workplace, there is an organizational goal or need that determines what is offered by learning and development and Kirkpatrick felt attention should be paid to whether or not that overarching need was satisfied.

Often, training sessions only assess participant reaction. While their satisfaction is important, learners can be satisfied with a session yet not learn from it or decide to use what was learned. Some have argued that satisfaction scores can be seen as a proxy for learning or behavior. Research has not borne this out; indeed, Warr et al. (1999) found that, although participant reactions were related to learning, they were generally unrelated to subsequent job behavior (Warr et al., 1999, p. 31, quoted in Tamkin et al., 2002). Dixon (1990) found no significant relationship between post-test scores and participants' perceptions of (a) the relevance of the course; (b) their own learning; (c) their enjoyment; or (d) the skill of the instructors. However, she did find significant correlations between participants' enjoyment and their ratings of the instructors. Despite these persistent findings, ratings of participant satisfaction remain the most common form of evaluation of workplace learning. Learning analytics hopes to change that.

"Learning Analytics is the science and art of gathering, processing, interpreting and reporting data related to the efficiency, effectiveness and business impact of development programs designed to improve individual and organizational performance and inform stakeholders" (Mattox et al., 2016, p. 13). An emerging data-science discipline, it develops analytical tools to better identify and implement measures of learning and development that enhance our understanding of what causes learning and how to support it. Siemens (2022) notes that complexity grows with increasing reliance on digital, social, and networked interconnectedness, and that networks are a dynamic context. He observes that learning occurs primarily in these networks: "It's networks all the way down." He adds, "If it's digital, it produces data. If you have data, you have analytics. Once you're in the space of analytics, you'll eventually get to AI." Siemens says:

> I think humanity stores its most complex knowledge in its cultural systems. And so, there's a lot that AI can do to aid us in our cognitive activities. But the cultural dynamics remain, if you will, the unique domain of human performance. (n.p.)

In many ways, this is one reason we emphasize creating a learning culture—it is a way to make learning part of the very DNA of the organization.

In learning analytics, as in all research, one of the most important steps is to ask the right questions. What do we need to know if we are going to improve the learning and development enterprise? This is a particularly difficult question since learning itself is not well understood. Gains in knowledge, skills, and attitudes can be assessed in classroom learning, but much learning today occurs on the job, is not highly conscious, interacts with changing conditions and other work-related factors, and is not amenable to baseline and post-intervention measurement. The challenge is even greater when we look at organization development since interventions occur over time, are multidimensional and multi-level, and call for collective rather than individual measures of change.

In the vignette that follows, Rob Perrone, head of learning analytics at a major professional services firm, notes that there is a political dimension to asking the right question.

BOX 9.1 REDEFINING THE VALUE PROPOSITION

Rob Perrone

Organizations are re-engaging with their culture and rebranding themselves post-pandemic. The identity of learning and development is being re-considered and newly aligned with our organization's brand. What is learning's value proposition now? How has it shifted? A few key moments have gotten us to this turning point.

The Previous Shift

Four years ago, prior to the pandemic, we began to consider how we could transform learning at our organization. We found from some of our data and analytics that people engaged in significant learning beyond what we offered. We refocused on providing a broader learning experience to our professionals. We invested in a new facility that paved the way for a new learning approach. We adopted a pull-versus-push concept, and began to think about a holistic learning architecture. It's not just formal learning. We looked at all these hours, all these courses we offered, and yet it was still not enough. So we began to explore, "Is what we are offering insufficient?"

At the time, our chief human resource officer was asking: How do we rethink that? Are we using the right mix of formal and informal learning? Are we properly blended? And that started the conversation around, "Are we really making an impact?" In addition, maybe what was insufficient was the data we were capturing. Satisfaction data was something you had to do, but it didn't shed light on the effectiveness of learning at all.

Our learning analytics were insufficient to make needed learning decisions. We had to go deeper, to look at other data available to us. We had to start looking at how we bring data together and start forming hypotheses the data can help inform. That kind of thinking changed the way we do learning analytics versus taking data that implied, "These satisfaction scores are good. That means the learning is good." This was flawed logic. We did a lot of qualitative research in those early stages. People told us about barriers to applying what they learned.

We began to look at other data sources including performance data, engagement data, data from managers and peers about whether or not someone changed after a learning experience. We triangulated all of these data sources to get at a deeper level of truth. So we started getting data from different sources to help us understand and make meaning of what was actually happening in a learning event. That was our evolution.

The hard sell was convincing leaders and the business that satisfaction scores aren't that important. We needed to ask bigger questions. I wanted to look at behavioral impact. I want to do more qualitative work, like Brinkerhoff's (2003) success case methods. Those are harder studies to do. You're only looking at one intervention using micro studies, but those are more meaningful and yield better decision making. They take a lot more of an investment. But that journey has taken us where we are now.

Disruption Number Two—COVID-19

When COVID-19 hit, everything was off the table. We reverted backwards. We had a big investment in a facility for face-to-face learning on which we had put all of our chips. But what were we going to do now that it was closed? Most of 2021 we worked on how to shift to virtual delivery. Our measurement also shifted, but in the wrong direction. It reverted back to number of assets and how much training was delivered. The success measure became questions such as, "Did you still grant the same number of credits? Did you have variable hours for people to choose from so they were able to continuously learn and have what they need?"

We strengthened the use of the virtual tools available to us, and invested in more technology because it became clear this is where we needed to be. Virtual took on a whole new life. Now that we have started returning to learning that is more social, collaborative, practice-focused, and hands-on in the networking community, you don't need to spend eight hours per day in a session. You work before the class online and then spend two days on site digging in and becoming connected with your peers and your colleagues. So we integrated what we learned from the digital pivot.

Shift 3—Returning to Impact

Now that we've emerged from a sole focus on virtual learning, we're starting to ask what learning analytics show this approach is working? Is this new way of thinking leading to better application on the job? From a learning analytics standpoint, it's about the structures we're setting up to determine if it's working or not. We want to understand the behavioral impact—are people using what they learned in a way that helps them do their job better?

Ethics Training—When Learning Analytics Works

To give an example of when I think learning analytics is done properly, I'll share the story of how we worked to transform ethics training. Some sanctions were made against us around our ethical decision making. This sent a shockwave through the organization. Our ethics are a differentiator, and then that came into question because people were doing the wrong thing for silly reasons. That is what got us involved in helping people really understand the role of learning analytics. Our regulators told us we needed to offer a certain number of hours of ethics training. But you can train someone in ethical decision making until they are blue in the face yet just because they are "trained" to do the right thing doesn't mean they are going to do it right when faced with an ethical decision.

I worked very closely with our learning leader on ethics and integrity to pull together a robust learning strategy that included measurement and evaluation at the core. We focused on a yearly cadence:

- Year One focused on foundational concepts so that everyone talked about ethics in the same way;
- Year Two was practical application;
- Year Three was about behaviors and solidifying a new culture; and
- Year Four was around monitoring, maintaining, and growing.

We set forth really strong Knowledge and Performance Indicators. We were very clear that learning is only a piece of the puzzle. Our regulators believed a certain number of hours of training would address the problem. We countered that we can answer some of the questions, but only if they are learning related. A much broader system is needed to get us to a better place. Because we set these indicators up front, we were able to track application of the training through on-the-job metrics. We redefined how we reported these data up the chain of command. This enabled us to talk about these kinds of data in leadership conversations. As a result, we got really good results with the ethics and integrity initiative.

Now in Year Three, people are using the learning activities and learning assets in moments of need, which wasn't happening before. For the learner, what's available at their fingertips to make a difficult conversation go better when they have to make tough ethical decisions is what is important. From a learning analytics standpoint, we are gathering those types of metrics (who's accessing what information) at the behavioral level. So in terms of Kirkpatrick's levels (1998), we're now focused beyond level two. We're looking at application (level three) and we're trying to get to more behavioral and business impact. Business impact is a lofty thing to measure, but we're scratching the surface. We talk about what an ethical business culture needs to look like, and learning metrics are contributing to defining that. What has really helped us is to say, "This isn't just our job; it's everybody's job. It's not just learning and development that can answer this question." And leadership has bought into that. These data have shown them that you're not going to solve the problem by doing a three-hour training program. I'm using ethics and integrity as an example because it's gone in the right direction. All along the way we have data and metrics that are showing what we're doing is working well or that we're not doing some things that need to be done.

A good example of how these metrics are useful is how data have helped address application on the job. We did a behavioral impact study of those who went through the Giving Voice to Values curriculum (Gentile, 2014) last year. A challenging barrier reported was not having a good script for what to say in these difficult conversations. So this year we took those data and focused on enablement and scripting. You can't write a script for every situation, but beyond the scripts we have developed from these data, we are also going to ask participants to provide us with their scripts—what have they used. Then we can add them to a database someone can search. If they are going to have an ethical conversation around retaliation, low performance, or discrimination, for example, they can search for a script or even a set of scripts that can be pulled together that they can use as a sounding board to prepare their own.

Asking the Right Question

The research questions we're trying to answer are becoming more sophisticated, and as they do, use of learning analytics is evolving. An important difference is that leaders are listening. For this example, sanctions caused leaders to pay attention. We pointed out that existing data would not really tell us what they wanted to know. It opened their eyes to ask whether the questions are the right ones. And when you have that push behind you and you have a learning leader who's willing to listen, you get that perfect storm. You have the outside saying you have to do something. The organization says this is important. You have a learning leader who's saying we're asking the wrong questions from our data. And then you have someone like me who's trying to push a little bit to say, we've got data, but we're not using it in the right way because we're not asking the right questions.

It's really all about asking the right research questions. We need to be clear about what problem we're trying to solve and how learning is going to contribute to that solution. If we're doing the right performance consulting up front, we've identified the performance gap, and we think learning is going to help bridge that gap—at that moment, that gray-line moment, is when we should be talking about the learning metrics that are going to be needed. As long as the research questions are positioned to address a performance gap and we can then collect the right analytics at the right level, then we have a good learning analytic structure in place.

That is harder to do when you don't have buy in at the top:

- when you don't have leaders who are focused on those questions;
- when you have people who are afraid of what that data might tell you about the system;
- when you don't want to go beyond that because the feel-good metrics have gotten you so far—promotions, money, budgets. You risk all of that. You put that on the line for higher-level metrics.

A good learning analytics leader or practitioner is one who can come in and say to leaders, "I'm not a judge. You want people to come and that's your measure of success. I'll get that data. If you want to put $1,000,000 into this program and you want ten people to come, that's your ROI. But that number is not your learning effectiveness number. They are not the same."

The discipline of designing your measurement and evaluation up front is key to doing the right thing. But people are slow to come to the table. Data are good for the business. But when it comes to your business, it's also like pulling back the covers a little bit. I'm not sure everyone wants to go there. The more we get to the right questions, the more we can show success stories, the more open minds people will have.

We always talk about VUCA. Why did we assume we (in learning and development) were immune to that? We're not. Sometimes a disruption is okay. It breaks everything up and makes you figure things out and come back together. The learner is my client. So I focus on that every day. I try to measure the impact of learning to them, to the organization, to the system and the group.

Perrone's example demonstrates that, to find and use analytics to the organization's advantage, rethinking L&D requires strong partnerships with the business to find and focus analytics on what matters most for business results. While some leaders may not want to ask the more difficult questions, others partner with learning analytics scholars to evolve more creative ways to measure the complex outcomes of learning and development efforts.

RETHINKING LEARNING ANALYTICS

Learning analytics has evolved considerably. With the increasing use of digital resources has come an array of data that can be mined to enhance the learning experience. LinkedIn Learning's Workplace Learning report of 2019 (LinkedIn Learning, 2019) noted that new measures of success of L&D are becoming more important, moving beyond satisfaction, simple participation, and seats filled. These new measures include looking at business impact and use of skills learned in one's work.

Joksimovic et al. (2020) note that an important area of growth in learning analytics is to move beyond measures focused on cognitive abilities to measures of social and emotional learning that are critical outcomes of learning and development.

Analytics for Informal Learning

Another emerging area of learning analytics looks at how informal learning can be captured and assessed. Ruiz-Calleja et al. (2017) note the previous lack of attention to informal learning in learning analytics and explains it thus: "One probable reason for this oversight is the fact that learning in the workplace is often informal, hard to grasp and not unequivocally defined" (p. 164).

DeLaat and Schreurs (2013) focus on the challenge of capturing informal learning in professional networks. It is a challenge because "[i]nformal learning activities are mostly implicit, ad hoc, spontaneous, and invisible to others .... As such, this problem presents an interesting challenge for the field of learning analytics (LA), namely, finding ways to capture and analyze traces of (social) informal learning in everyday life and work networks" (p. 1422).

Social network analysis is often used to try to capture some of this learning. However, while this approach can look at the density and degree of connection between individuals in a network, "[t]hese statistics tell us a lot about how information is shared through network relationships, but this says little or nothing about how and what is being learned" (DeLaat and Schreurs, 2013, p. 1423).

Networked learning theory offers some light on how networks become vehicles for learning. Bieke and Maarten (2012) view networked learning as a kind of informal learning situated in practice. They note that this type of learning is growing and as a consequence,

> As more and more people participate in multiple networks—learning by observation in some, and participating strongly in others—extending the scope of learning to include lean and rich engagement in social networks is becoming more important for understanding individual experience in a multi-dimensional, multi-membership,

Table 9.1 *Support for workplace informal learning processes*

Informal learning behavior	Definition	Social network implications
Help seeking, guidance and support	"the processes in which individuals seek, provide and find support from collective knowledge (social networking and community technologies)" (p. 1045)	Knowledge generated can be shared with others
Task performance, reflection and sensemaking	"the processes of experiencing, reflecting about, sharing and collectively validating the learning moments connected with task performance" (p. 1044)	Recording reflections in the situated context and in the moment may enhance individual and potentially collective sensemaking
Emergence and maturing of collective knowledge	"describe how individual learning interactions, their traces and related materials are made available to others" (p. 1045)	"When others are made aware of these via social networking and community technologies, individual uptake or a broader negotiation in a community setting can occur. This can then trigger processes of co-creation and knowledge maturing in which materials are refined and developed into more mature cultural artifacts and made available for a wider target group" (p. 1046)

Source: Adapted from Ley et al., 2014.

> and multi-identity world. Informal Learning thus engages with a wider view of the influences and impacts on [an] individual's ideas and knowledge acquisition, a view that is synergistic with the greater availability of information and social contacts accompanying developments on the Internet in an increasingly networked society. (p.62)

Ley et al. (2014) look at three informal workplace learning processes and how they can be supported with technology: (1) task performance, reflection, and sensemaking; (2) help seeking, guidance, and support; and (3) emergence and maturing of collective knowledge. The authors focus particularly on learning within networks or communities of practice. The informal learning processes that can be assisted and captured using technology are described in Table 9.1.

USING QUALITATIVE EVALUATION APPROACHES

Program evaluators have long used mixed methods approaches to evaluate educational programs, but qualitative research has been less often used in L&D. Some evaluators are hoping to change that. For example, Robert Brinkerhoff

(2005) proposed using a qualitative success case method to take a more whole organizational approach. A developmental approach holds particular promise.

A study by Watkins et al. (2011) used a developmental evaluation model (Patton, 2011), a theory of change approach (Evaluation Forum, 2003), and critical incident interviews (Flanagan, 1954) to identify individual and organizational outcomes of an emerging managers' leadership development program that used an action learning approach. As O'Neil and Marsick (2007) note, "When participants work on workplace problems in action learning programs, they not only learn by doing but they also come face-to-face with the messy, ambiguous reality that often exists outside the classroom" (quoted in Watkins et al., 2011, p. 215) Characteristics of this kind of L&D required a different analytic.

Watkins et al. (2011) note,

> Existing evaluation models ... were designed to capture learning in fairly traditional training formats based on fixed objectives. Increasingly, leadership development is much more holistic, focused on challenging experiences, knowledge acquisition, skill development, and solving real business problems as in action learning-based leadership development ... Embedded in these complex program designs are opportunities for individuals and their managers to self-identify outcomes; and for serendipitous outcomes to emerge from the experiences, the settings selected, and the challenges faced. What is needed is a more robust approach that examines changes that impact both the individual and the organization. (p. 209)

The researchers captured critical incidents of new behavior on the job from participants and from their managers. This multi-level view validated participant perspectives but also demonstrated that supervisors often saw new behavior before the participants themselves had fully assimilated the changes they'd experienced. Using a theory of change model of evaluation (Evaluation Forum, 2003) allowed the researchers to identify outcomes from the development initiative at multiple levels—from the individual, to the unit, to the organization and over time. Interviews were conducted at six months and one year after the action learning program concluded. This allowed enough time for them to identify whether or not changes were embedded in the managers' daily work.

Watkins et al. (2011) noted, "leaders rapidly absorb new learning and make it part of their everyday routines. Qualitative approaches such as these conducted over time help draw a clearer picture of what learning looks like at each stage" (p. 234). At the same time, the interviews themselves served as a learning intervention.

Watkins et al. (2011) assert, "evaluation processes must mirror the complexity found in programs based on open and often intangible outcomes and focus on organizational capacity building more than on fixed objectives" (p. 215).

They see that the "complexity of commingled individual and organizational outcomes and learning capacities that vary by whatever previous capacities individuals and organizations brought to the development activity requires us to rethink evaluation of emerging program outcomes, focusing on change at different levels" (p. 215). The value of a qualitative approach is in the power of the narrative to help leaders and program designers actually see what transpired.

By describing the learning in participants' own words, leaders develop a grounded understanding of what is actually learned from programs such as these. While data on participant satisfaction with the program and attainment of objectives are valuable, higher-level outcomes such as cognitive re-construal, identity shifts, and organizational impacts are unlikely to be readily quantifiable—nor even necessarily predictable. The open-ended nature of qualitative interviews permits a wider exploration and illuminates unanticipated and important outcomes (Watkins et al., 2011, p. 235).

PEOPLE ANALYTICS—AND L&D

This chapter would not be complete without addressing people analytics. These data are not directly focused on enhancing L&D delivery. They do nudge employees to enroll in L&D programs, identify missing competencies for which L&D might provide new programs to address, and generally capture and mine data about the talent in the organization. People analytics was defined by Tursunbayeva et al. (2018) as:

> an area of HRM practice, research and innovation concerned with the use of information technologies, descriptive and predictive data analytics and visualisation tools for generating actionable insights about workforce dynamics, human capital, and individual and team performance that can be used strategically to optimise organizational effectiveness, efficiency and outcomes, and improve employee experience. (p. 231)

Learning and development has been called the last frontier of people analytics since it is widely used in finance, operations, logistics, and other areas of the organization. In human resources, people analytics have been used to mine through thousands of applications to identify best fit for particular positions, to sort among higher and lower performing employees to identify potential training opportunities, to identify high-risk employees to prevent turnover, etc. (de Romrée et al., 2016). Yet data have also been used to monitor eye movements, attention, distraction, and other variables in on-line learning; to monitor remote work, and to select talent in ways that sometimes avoid gender and racial bias, and other times increase it. Not surprisingly, a significant stream of research in people analytics is thus devoted to the ethical considerations of using these data.

Asking the right questions as in all evaluation is critical. Through data analysis, deeper underlying correlations can be uncovered that point the way to more strategic interventions. A case study of the use of data analytics to drive the turnaround of a high turnover retail business, fast food, led to four key interventions that contradicted prevailing management beliefs about what was leading to turnover. Using personality assessments, an assessment of organizational health, extensive employee and store data, researchers at McKinsey were able to test over a hundred hypotheses about what was and was not working and the relationships between employee behavior and store outcomes (Arellano et al., 2017). Findings included such things as shift length (6 hours was optimal though management had been giving longer shifts to reduce commute time), personality traits (a focus on getting the job done was more important than an outgoing personality contrary to management belief), and management contact (presence of which was critical). Interventions were designed around these findings; results four months into the pilot were that customer satisfaction increased by 100%, profits were up 5%, and retention of new hires was higher. These results suggest that it is not only the mining of data that is important; new data that can illuminate these key relationships might be needed.

In a similar study, Jinks and Watkins (2020) conducted a study to predict intent to remain in a fast food chain with over 200% employee turnover. They hypothesized that access to informal learning opportunities, engagement, and a learning culture would correlate with intent to remain. The model developed explained over 50% of the overall variability in intent to remain with the chain. The predictor variable, learning culture, was the most influential variable, explaining over 29% of variability. Studies such as these can confirm the importance of L&D initiatives, for example whether to focus on creating a learning culture or supporting employee engagement. They also point to important differences among employees that enable L&D to target their efforts. For example, in the Jinks and Watkins study, there was a significant difference between high- and low-wage employees, with low-wage employees much more likely to be retained in stores with a strong learning culture, while higher-wage employees were less impacted by the strength of the learning culture. In addition, this organization invested heavily in employee engagement initiatives, yet this turned out to be less impactful on intent to remain than the learning culture. This finding suggests a refocus of the engagement initiative.

ETHICS IN PEOPLE ANALYTICS

Giermindl et al. (2022) look at the dark side of people analytics. They observe these assumptions made by advocates of people analytics: "firstly, people analytics is more objective and less error-prone than human decision making, and secondly, based on historical data, it is able to predict future human behaviour" (p. 414). The authors note that neither of these is necessarily so. They explore a number of potential challenges in using people analytics found in a review of the literature. We highlight a few of them here. Human error is certainly one of the more crucial ones. They state:

> One common theme emerging from these studies is that HR [human resources] professionals often lack the required analytics capabilities .... Because data do not speak for themselves, HR managers have to decide which questions to ask, how to interpret and make sense of the findings, put the results in perspective, and draw conclusions from the data. (p. 415)

Lack of ability to ask good questions or to interpret the data are made more difficult by the sheer volume of this type of data. In addition, it can also lead to poorly trained or inaccurate algorithms. As in any study, garbage in, garbage out. How the algorithm is programmed takes considerable understanding of the output needed and the data available.

Compared to data in other domains, people analytics generate more moral and ethical concerns due to the very personal, often intrusive nature of this data (Giermindl et al., 2022). In one's private life, an individual may opt out of sharing their private data. In an organization, they cannot do so; and they often have no idea what data are being tracked or how they will be used. How they are used can be highly consequential to individuals, targeting them for promotion, or potentially for less desirable consequences:

> The majority of these studies raised privacy and data protection concerns that result from increasingly intrusive actions of people analytics .... These studies stress that employees face more and more invasive information collection, processing and dissemination as the people analytics boundaries are progressively extended from employees' work lives into their social and even physiological spaces. Such intrusion was found to evoke negative responses and resistance from employees and to hamper their commitment. (Giermindl et al., 2022, p. 418)

Leonardi and Contractor (2018) argue that people analytics have been more hype than reality. They use social network analysis, what they call relational analytics, to identify employees more likely to innovate, to influence, etc., by analyzing "digital exhaust"—the e-mails, Microsoft Teams connections, and other digital evidence of connections. They argue for this kind of passive data collection as less demanding of employee time than surveys that are often used to identify who is talking to, or working with, whom. Yet, they also admit that this can be seen as an invasion of privacy and ask that organizations are transparent when using this kind of data. That these data might be misused seems equally likely with many, if not most, unable to meaningfully interpret the importance of the social relations of employees.

That employees react negatively to such intrusive tactics is not surprising, but the level of monitoring possible continues to escalate. Constant tracking and collecting ever more granular data affects employees' sense of autonomy. Use of these data for decision making may undermine managers' authority and can even impede their ability to support decisions since they do not know the rationale behind the data collected or the accuracy of that data. As Giermindl et al. (2022) note,

> Overall, if the deployed learning algorithms and AI function as a black box, it seems difficult to determine who can be held accountable for serious mistakes, significant failures, and misconduct of a system .... Such opacity can create information asymmetries, obscure power structures and inhibit oversight, as well as negatively influence workers' perceived procedural fairness and organisational commitment. (Giermindl et al., 2022, p. 424)

The authors give an example of this:

> For example, at the Siemens factory in Congleton, a software called Preactor was introduced to give the workshop teams instructions on which parts to produce and in what order. Rather than relying on their human judgment and experience, workers now receive a specific set of instructions from the software telling them exactly in what order to perform each step. While the cell managers welcomed the clarity and simplicity of the production and action plans, production workers complained about their loss of autonomy and the devaluation of their skills and knowledge. The algorithmic decision templates stepped in, compromising the former social relationships between management and production employees and making it impossible for managers to adequately assess the new system's negative effects on employees. (Giermindl et al., 2022, p. 427)

Gal et al. (2020) identify three pitfalls of algorithmic management: opacity, datafication of the workforce, and nudging to incentivize certain behaviors. To mitigate the negative effects of people analytics, the authors call for a fostering of new mindsets—including thinking of people analytics as a fallible companion to decision making, and building skills in monitoring algorithms and exploring their effect on the people in the organization. In addition, redesigning the algorithmic system itself to publish confidence levels will help to determine how confident we should be about the accuracy of the data or redesigning the system to act more like an executive assistant:

> The aim of an expert assistant is not to push us into action based on predefined evaluation criteria, but to facilitate reflection, ask questions, give hints, propose alternative options—thereby cultivating our ability to identify and assess the moral consequences of different options, act voluntarily, and develop practical wisdom. (p. 11)

People analytics will continue to creep into the L&D function. It is therefore imperative that L&D professionals are aware of both the potential and the challenges of these algorithmic tools. They have the potential to enable practitioners to look at enormous amounts of data and to find hitherto hidden relationships that can reveal more effective ways to guide learning and development. Designing their use ethically and with considerable care for both the impact on the learner and for their usefulness in providing accurate actionable knowledge will be the new skill frontier for L&D. Determining when and what to measure to advance L&D will continue to be a significant challenge.

10. Continuing reflections

This book has depicted learning and development (L&D) in transition as human beings grapple with complexity. These portraits and perspectives—snapshots of change in time and context, but by no means the whole of the shifting terrain—are points on a scattergram. We depended on literature reviews for painting the big picture. We tapped a "snowball" sample of well-known global icons and professional services organizations; these responded to our invitation for in-depth illustrations. Context is everything in complexity, and as Renee Rogers, an OD practitioner describing her organization's learning journey, opined: "More will always be revealed" (in Marsick & Watkins, 1999, p. 16).

The pandemic—coupled with the digitally driven Fourth Industrial Revolution and contextual changes—has stimulated unlearning, learning, and relearning through facing disturbance. "Disturbance drives evolution." And because "ecosystems do not exhibit firm causality," we do not look for predictable trends, but rather, propensities. "Propensities are *tendencies* to act in a particular way given an entity's capacities" (Pendleton-Jullian & Brown, 2018a, p. 37). The patterns detected are propensities. They do not tell the whole story of L&D's evolution. They offer a window into pioneer footsteps and possible futures.

Throughout our interviews with chief learning officers and other senior L&D managers, we have heard the words "Integration," "Adaptation," and "Purpose." Other patterns we have heard/seen have to do with design and practices: democratization of learning via learner experience and learner-driven approaches, machine and Artificial Intelligence (AI) as partners in learning, L&D leaders questioning assumptions about learning and design, intrinsic motivation (pull), peer learning, and creation spaces. Entangled with integration is the questioning of fundamental assumptions about learning as well as design assumptions, for example: What is learning? Don't people learn naturally when they pursue their goals? Does all learning have to be interactive? How can we integrate digital learning approaches with more traditional classroom-based training? How can we integrate learning in an organizational culture initiative? What business software can we re-purpose to serve the learning function? How can we use an innovation design tool to develop, disseminate, rate, and revise solutions to wicked problems? How can we use a community of practice platform to support post-training implementation and use? How can we re-purpose sales and customer service AI software to

Table 10.1 *L&D's evolution*

From	To
Upskilling	Reskilling
Behaviorist approaches to learning	Situated cognition, connectivism
Separation of personal and work interests	Bringing the whole self to work
Acculturation to "how things are done"	Honoring diverse employee ways of being
Credentials based on knowledge	Skills that are validated
Transmitting knowledge	Creating knowledge
Individual focus	Collaborative, relational focus
Individual unit of analysis	Group, organizational, social network unit of analysis
Face to face primarily	Digital delivery primarily
Manager, HR directed learning	Democratizing learning options
ADDIE instructional design	Design unbound
Formal learning predominantly	Informal, incidental, and formal learning though increasingly IIL
Library of learning assets	A learning culture
L&D as a solo function	Integrated with organization development, human resources, talent management
Satisfaction, seats filled as only metrics	Impact, more holistic metrics

Source: Authors.

automate reminders, announcements, nudges, etc., to support the learning and development function? How can we use learning to help us understand and enhance the employee experience of key organizational visions and values? How can we align the yardsticks we use to measure learning and development outcomes with the organization's mission and purposes? These are some of the challenges learning and development professionals confront.

Professionals are responding in creative ways to these challenges. We have moved from one iteration of learning and development to another—and yet in many ways, we are actually adding capacities rather than giving up traditional approaches to L&D. Some of the changes we have seen include those in Table 10.1.

CHALLENGES FACING L&D PRACTITIONERS

Questions of control, power dynamics, and conscious or implicit bias continue to trouble L&D and human resource development (HRD). Scaffolding enables the organization to nudge, guide,. and shape learning in the flow of work to leverage intrinsic motivation and energy-expanding experimentation. The shadow side of capturing and exploiting the power of learning in the workflow can be exploitation and surveillance, given the capacities of technology and data analytics to track employees' online work and reward primarily that which can be tracked, that is, work done on technology versus investment in human relationship building and interactions. We are in the early period of rosy estimation of the opportunities that may arise by partnering with intelligent technologies and supporting learning that is driven by intrinsic motivation. While we know curiosity and energy are released by positive psychology, it would be naive to ignore cautions prompted by the history of management–labor relations, discrimination, and other negative forces at work.

One area of focus going forward will be whether or not, and how, control of learning choices and directions are shared with learners. Poell et al. (2000) noted that "employees are frequently disregarded as (co-)organizers of their own learning processes" (p. 26). They support learning networks that arise more frequently in flattened organizations. Employees' learning paths differ by who takes initiative or action for learning, how the process is carried out, and what learning structures or "stable patterns" emerge for support (Poell et al., 2018).

But how do L&D practitioners develop themselves? Certainly academic programs such as ours that focus on workplace L&D have played a key role in professionalizing L&D (Watkins & Marsick, 2016), and professional associations have provided ongoing professional development. An intriguing professional development opportunity for workplace L&D professionals is that provided at Harvard University.

SHOES FOR THE SHOEMAKER'S CHILDREN

Where do chief learning officers go to rethink learning strategies and identify next practices for human development? One trailblazer for collaborative learning tied to pressing, current workplace learning challenges is the Learning and Innovation Laboratory (LILA) based at the Harvard Graduate School of Education. LILA was founded in 2000 by principal investigators David Perkins and Daniel Wilson. It is one of many research projects under Project Zero, the longest continuously operating project within Harvard. The research laboratory is a member-based learning community that comes together multiple times per year to learn, to share current challenges, and explore strategic initiatives amid the complexity of members' different contexts. LILA has three goals: to craft intellectual insights, to foster practical application, and to create social connections. Every interaction is intentionally designed to support these goals. LILA convenes three two-day gatherings, a two-day learning summit, five member calls, and two focused interview sessions, along with frequent additional contact throughout a given year. Membership deliberately includes non-competing organizations in the for-profit, non-profit, and governmental sectors. Representative participants at these sessions are responsible for the strategic initiatives that lead to nurturing human and organizational learning. They typically hold titles like Learning Officer, People Officer, Head of Transformation, and Head of Talent. What makes the laboratory unique is their deliberate and thoughtful experimentation around generating learning conversations prompted by members' own learning agendas.

BOX 10.1 CREATING A GENERATIVE LEARNING COMMUNITY FOR LEARNING AND DEVELOPMENT LEADERS

Marga Biller, Senior Project Director, Learning and Innovation Laboratory (LILA), Harvard Graduate School of Education

In this vignette, I describe some of the ways in which LILA aims to create and nurture a learning community for senior leaders of organizations. A core mission of LILA is to create the space for learning from and with one another in order to collectively make sense of the year's theme and to identify opportunities to translate research into practice. This begins with a community conversation around potential themes for the year. Once a theme is selected, we invite researchers to join us as guest speakers and share their work with LILA members. Given the complex nature of the themes we take on, the academics we invite represent a variety of disciplines.

By introducing different voices and perspectives, we push our thinking into new areas. The faculty members who participate in LILA may have direct links to a theme like Ecologies of Learning; for example, Karen Watkins and Victoria Marsick, who have spent their professional careers investigating learning and development. We also invite researchers in "adjacent areas," such as political scientist Michael Kenney (University of Pittsburg), who studies terrorism, Islamist militancy, and transnational organized crime. Criminal and extremist groups have to be adaptable to their environments and update and transfer knowledge often. They have created learning ecologies that support their culture and operations, even if they don't call them that. At LILA we expand our understanding of the theme and how to operationalize ideas by bringing in multiple perspectives that push our thinking and drive us to find our "learning edge."

As our members' roles changed, we expanded the focus of our themes from traditional learning and development topics to include organizationally related, strategic themes. We have also moved from involving mostly US-based researchers to a more global reach. That's valuable—not just because the research and approaches are different, but because the places where these academics are conducting research represent different contexts and challenges. It gets us out of our echo chambers.

Our Process

Generating annual themes

When the LILA team begins deliberations regarding potential themes for the upcoming year, we consider the challenges member organizations are facing, identify current research that might inform our exploration, and keep in mind the personal interests of the members and the team. The team writes up sketches of the themes, reviews them and finally proposes three themes to members during the last member call of the year. The LILA team consolidates the feedback, identifies where the cohort's energy lies, and makes a decision about next year's theme. At the last gathering of the year, the LILA Summit, the theme for the following year's cycle is shared with the broader LILA community and beyond.

Selecting LILA faculty

We aim for six different faculty guests who will be part of three gatherings (two faculty per gathering), plus seven faculty guests for the Summit, and five academics who will share their work during member calls. I set up an initial conversation with them to learn more about their research, how it would apply to LILA members' challenges and initiatives, and what practical connections they see between their research and the real-world challenges faced by member organizations. We ask faculty to be a part of the community for the entirety of the two days of each of the gatherings, taking part in the conversation cafés and learning rounds.

Surfacing member's challenges

During our hour-long conversation, we identify members' big organizational challenges, the initiatives LILA members are leading, and specific questions they are thinking about that, if answered through the year-long exploration, would help them make progress on their challenges. Interviews are summarized and shared with the rest of the LILA community. This process helps guide each member's learning journey through the year. We revisit these conversations halfway through the year and prompt them to think about, "What have you learned so far, what do you still want to explore?" Other members in the trio being interviewed add their voices and raise questions or share ideas. A lot of richness and learning occurs in these follow-up calls.

The gatherings

Our yearly cycle encompasses four two-day gatherings, each one focused on a different topic that together make up the learning arc. While members share practices that have worked in their organizations, they come to LILA to explore how the primary research shared by academics can inform their approach to the challenges they are facing. The four sessions are designed to introduce research related to the theme, make connections between the research and members' challenges, and create opportunities for collective sensemaking and discovery.

The last gathering of the year, the LILA Summit, is the culmination of our year-long exploration. To date, we have hosted more than 96 gatherings over the course of 22 years. We invite not just current members to the Summit, but anyone who has been a member or faculty over the 20-plus years of LILA. Although we strategically limit the yearly membership in LILA to no more than 25 organizations, the Summit could range between 60 and 100 participants. Day one of the Summit expands the community and combines new and previous voices. The Summit highlights the research of a keynote speaker, and of six past faculty members who lead small group sessions about recent research. Day two is for members only to consolidate the learning over the year.

Member calls

In the months between the gatherings, we hold five member conference calls during which additional LILA faculty guests provide input based on what has garnered energy during each of the gatherings. Member calls continue the conversations from the gatherings and nudge members to keep thinking about the ideas and to experiment with them.

Scaffolding Learning and Enhancing Professional Practices

Given that the yearly thematic arcs LILA explores are complex and require a multidisciplinary approach, the LILA team keeps this question top of mind: How can we best support the learning that happens within the community as well as the impact the learning can bring both at the individual level and to support the organizational initiatives our members are leading? Two of the practices we use to foster learning and impact members' practices follow.

Learning conversations

Paying attention to how to foster learning conversations is at the heart of what we do. We take the "laboratory" part of the project's name seriously and constantly introduce small changes to enhance the nature of these conversations. For example, Daniel Wilson, co-Principal Investigator of LILA, led a research study in which he and his team identified learning outcomes and explored what led to that learning. The findings suggested there are three conversation moves that make for more productive learning conversations: Asking Questions, Taking a Provocative Point of View, and Sharing a Personal Story.

Thinking routines

Thinking routines were developed across a number of research projects at Project Zero. A thinking routine is a set of questions or steps used to scaffold thinking. We use a thinking routine for sensemaking comprising three steps: Insights, Puzzles, and Actions (IPAs). After engaging in a free-flowing conversation in small sensemaking groups, members consolidate their thinking by listing Insights, Puzzles, and Actions.

Learning from and with one another

Learning communities thrive when participants learn from and about the people around us. This requires a high degree of vulnerability in identifying what we don't yet know, sharing it with trusted others, and asking for help. LILA aims to create a place for this type of learning to occur. One example is the learning rounds.

Learning rounds

LILA learning rounds are based on the medical school model of "rounds," where doctors, residents, and other staff come together to share knowledge and practice clinical diagnostic skills. These 45-minute learning rounds are integrated into the LILA learning ecology and are a key component of learning from and with one another.

To illustrate the value of learning rounds, one example stands out. Jim Martin, Dean at the Army Staff College and Chief Academic Officer at the Army University, shared a challenge that took place when combat for the troops shifted from tanks in large formations to small groups of soldiers that became part of local communities and worked with the citizens to make things happen. Jim and his staff had to completely rethink what and how they were teaching their commanders. At the time, the Army University had 63 different schools. Jim was wondering, what should be centralized? What should be decentralized? Each school was very territorial, adding to the challenge. One of the LILA members that year was at the YMCA. During the learning round, the senior leader from the YMCA described their franchise operating model. The YMCA serves the local community and must tailor the curriculum to the needs of each community. Each community has freedom in certain curriculum and programmatic choices, but not in others.

Jim's "Aha!" moment came about as a result of the input from the YMCA member. He found that thinking about the change they were trying to effect through the franchise lens was a total game changer as he started to re-envision their curriculum development process, and even the way curriculum was implemented, shifting from a headquarters mindset to a franchise model.

I work with the member who is bringing their challenge to craft a two-page briefing document, shared in advance with members. I meet with the member bringing the challenge to flesh it out and to clarify: What's the real challenge here? What are the three questions you want the group to take on? What have you tried so far, and what's worked? What hasn't worked? Why is this important to the organization now? And if you were successful, what would be different?

We facilitate two learning rounds concurrently. Members read both briefing documents in advance, then choose which to attend. During the session we use the "step back process" developed by Robert Kegan of the Harvard Graduate School of Education. Once an initial clarification step is concluded, participants sit in a circle. The member who brought the challenge sits just outside the circle as a physical reminder not to partake in this conversation but to listen, learn, and think about which ideas they want to explore further. The facilitator guides the process to prompt generative conversations. Midway, the facilitator asks, "Are we having the conversation you want us to be having? Is there something you've heard that you want us to dig into deeper, or do you want to redirect the conversation?"

When we have run the course for the learning round, we provide a few minutes to the person who brought the challenge and ask, "Can you think about one or two ideas that were most provocative for you that you can bring back to the members and share the learning?" And we also ask the members, "Of all the ideas you heard, which do you think the learning round host should consider?" This helps all participants consolidate their ideas. Learning happens on both sides.

Turning Ideas into Practice

Each LILA gathering generates an abundance of learning nuggets. Part of the challenge is to identify how this learning could be converted into organizational or individual practices. Below are two examples of how we support members turning ideas into practice.

So Now What cafés

These small group conversations that take place towards the end of our gatherings are specifically designed to promote the practical application of the ideas generated at LILA. Members explore how they can experiment with the ideas presented.

LILA "tarot" cards
One of the experiments LILA created to support turning ideas to practice was the LILA "tarot cards." After each gathering, the LILA team identifies the key ideas generated and creates an actionable card that could be used by a LILA member to promote a discussion about the concept and spread the learning back to their organization. Tarot cards include a graphic image from the session depicting the idea, a concise description of the idea, and ways to apply the idea.

Generating Learning Artifacts

Throughout LILA gatherings and calls, members identify insights, puzzles, and actions. A team of Harvard Master's students document all of the conversations and presentations, as well as a resident graphic recorder. They create two learning artifacts I highlight below.

Harvest documents
Detailed summaries of each LILA gathering are compiled into a "harvest document" that is shared with members. Members are encouraged to share this document within their organizations to spread the ideas further. All of the harvest documents from the gatherings are accessible to members through the LILA website so they can review relevant ideas from previous years that might help inform their initiatives.

Graphic images
Sita Magnuson of Dpict, our graphic recorder, is an incredibly talented synthesizer who creates appealing graphics that capture the ideas faculty share at LILA as well as LILA members' sensemaking. These images are physically present in the room when we meet in person and visible online when we meet virtually. We deliberately create moments for members to interact with the graphic images as a way to recall ideas, share ideas, and note connections.

Final Reflection

We have learned a lot over the 20-plus years of LILA about what it takes to create, nurture, and support a learning community, and much of it happens through the conversations the LILA team engages in and the way in which we approach serving the needs of the community. Our commitment is to create a place where professionals from diverse organizations and backgrounds can come together to seek ideas about how to make organizations places where those who choose to work in them can have a sense of agency, feel a sense of belonging, and create meaningful connections to each other. LILA is a place where you can find inspiration that helps you hone your craft and nourish your soul.

As is evident in this vignette, learning communities may evolve spontaneously, but great care and structuring can make them much more powerful. We next highlight characteristics of complex systems discussed in this book. We explore ways to work with and within complex environments, given that they cannot be managed or controlled because they are unpredictable.

WORKPLACE LEARNING & COMPLEXITY

Complex systems can alter their operations and remain resilient over time, continuing to perform at a high level in the presence of changing environmental conditions. How has the growing complexity of the learning context affected L&D? We have suggested a number of possible ways L&D has responded to different degrees of complexity. Figure 10.1 depicts a way of thinking about this.

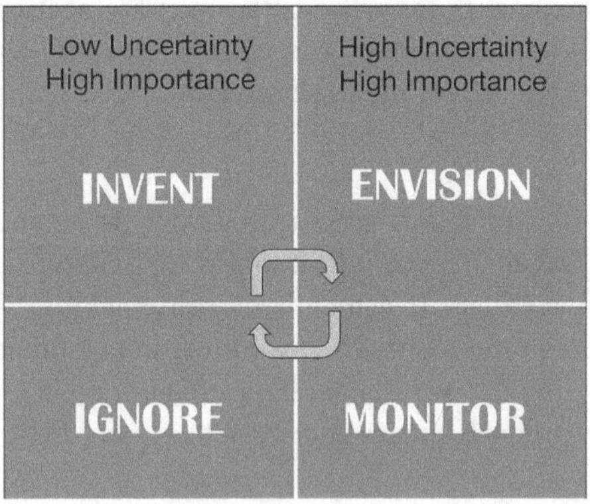

Source: K. E. Watkins.

Figure 10.1 The uncertainty matrix

Faced with uncertainty, we navigate the situation differently depending on how important it is to respond. In a situation of high uncertainty but low importance, we need only monitor it to see if something occurs to which we do need to formulate a response. But if the situation is of high uncertainty and high importance, there is no clear direction forward, and so we have to draw on our abductive imagination to envision possibilities that are currently unknown to us, what Scharmer (2009) calls presencing. Similarly, Snowden and Boone's (2007) Cynefin framework suggests that in complex contexts, leaders need to probe, sense, and respond—get information about the situation, make sense of it, and determine a way to act. We have seen both of these approaches in these pages—Unilever envisioning a way to provide future jobs for their employees, ESPN probing concerns about equity and finding collective ways to respond.

Learning in complex systems cannot be centrally planned, although L&D can partner with business units and create a rich environment for learning. L&D designers in this book opted for decentralization. For example, IBM and Unilever created learner-centered digital pathways to upskill and/or reskill employees that entice employees to retool themselves for the digital economy. Unilever, however, did not leave motivation to chance. They agreed with recent thinking that purpose—what drives and pulls us forward—is an essential ingredient for success. So Unilever helped employees to discover their purpose and use it to guide reskilling. Complex learning environments also assume that employees know how to learn, but that is not always the case. Rethinking L&D might involve practices such as learning communities to collaboratively address situated challenges (Jimenez, 2019). Learning and knowledge can be structured into work practices as well, as illustrated by agile teaming practices or, on a smaller scale, tools to aid boundary crossing in teams.

Control in complex systems is not centralized; it is distributed and local—reflecting the push toward decentralizing learning and putting it in the hands of learners. Rules for adaptation and change are local and simple. Yet, in interaction and interdependence with others, complex patterns may emerge by use of simple rules. ESPN began with simple conversations about what made people feel included in the culture and ended in such conversations being part of the culture. Individual agents act interdependently in consonance with local rules.

Regularities develop spontaneously over time in response to changes in agents' surrounding conditions. Patterns emerge that are properties of the system as a whole. Pattern feedback further influences agent interactions. In this way, small moves can have outsized, unexpected consequences. An example: The Geneva Learning Foundation's scaffolded combination of dialogue groups formed around content with ad hoc, paired, shared experiences across geopolitical as well as hierarchical medical professional boundaries. Tools such as "hackathons" and the "idea engine" were further used to stimulate knowledge creation rather than passive reliance on outmoded, dysfunctional, "banking approach" (Freire, 1970) teaching.

Although statistically rare, a metaphorically "catastrophic" state can occur at any time—with desired or undesired effect; hence, the need for learning from small experiments to test options even while recognizing a next precarious state could be around the corner. As well, this precarity shows the value of empowered distributed leadership—based on the assumption that no single leader can understand and act in complex circumstances solely on their own. The German ICU unit vignette that follows (Box 10.2) shows how a hospital structured and staffed operations in order to monitor recovery of patients in complex circumstances. This intentional design of checks and balances minimized risks of acting prematurely on the wrong conclusions that might have led to patient avalanches. We contrast the German example with a US COVID-19 ICU example to illustrate the power of structure, culture, and mandated practices to shape learning and decision making.

BOX 10.2 LEARNING IN COMPLEX HEALTHCARE SYSTEMS

Peter Neaman, Medical Communications, Right Angle

Uncertainty Management in a German ICU

The staff and management of a ten-bed German intensive care unit in a multidisciplinary intensive care unit (ICU) in a university hospital used structures and practices to maintain optimal care in the face of the unexpected in complex clinical cases (Schreyögg & Ostermann, 2014). As the ICU is characterized by high processual density and intense time pressure, situations that are dangerous—and unexpected—call for medical management adaptations.

Patients needing immediate care after cardiac surgery are the ICU's primary clientele. However, patients in a very critical state are also admitted from other medical disciplines such as urology, gynecology, "ear-nose-&-throat" when beds are available. Patients may also develop multiple problems (e.g., pneumonia and/or multiple organ failure) so that many medical disciplines can be involved. This ICU, then, is a prime example of how to proceed effectively in an organizational unit where staff members have to deal with great uncertainty and the unexpected on a regular basis.

Two types of patient management situations are encountered. First, some cases—whether complicated or not—are relatively routine in this unit for patients from any medical specialty. These can usually be handled with standardized protocols that are applied only to the management of conditions characterized by "known unknowns." The focus of management adaptation—and of this vignette—is primarily on managing classically complex cases that challenge care by sudden and/or unexpected manifestations of "unknown unknowns."

In a summary way, the adaptations pursued reflect recommendations of Weick and Sutcliffe (2015):

- consider the ICU an uncertainty management unit (p. 23),
- be reluctant to simplify ("Don't dumb down the complexity") (p. 63),
- simplify—i.e., place your initial raw perception into a conceptual "category" by expressing it in words as late as possible; and don't "combine it in your mind" with others' verbal opinions, until it becomes necessary to ACT! (p. 71),
- self-organize into ad hoc networks to obtain expert problem solving (p. 138),
- make sure the unexpected is noticed and considered before it can lead to catastrophic consequences (p. 22),
- keep asking yourself what's different (p. 72).

Adaptation Mechanisms in the German ICU

Reducing uncertainty

In most medical organizations there are clear-cut hierarchical structures—demarcated by titles, duties, and responsibilities. These lines of command and control are utilized for all usual decision-making processes. When necessary, decisions are escalated or delegated up hierarchy to the corresponding level of responsibility.

However, when unexpected incidents occur, hierarchical structures are temporarily suspended, and hierarchy is bypassed. Informal communication and expert networks come to the fore (Schreyögg & Ostermann, 2014). This holds true for cross-level-and-departmental communication as well as coordination between physicians and nurses. Schreyögg and Ostermann found that formal hierarchy is replaced by a hidden hierarchy of expertise that comes to the fore in unexpected situations.

Physicians draw extensively on networks for cooperative consultation, which consist of members inside and outside their units and even extra-organizational experts. It is common to seek advice from colleagues from other departments or units to obtain their ideas on an unexpected case. Preference is for experts already known to the physician seeking advice.

Monitoring and Promoting Uncertainty

Another distinctive feature in the German ICU is that, because it is an uncertainty *management* unit, this combination of formal organizational structure and informal practices—as well as inquiry by medical personnel at upper levels—is not only designed to reduce uncertainty, but also to induce it. Several of the above-described mechanisms provide a twofold effect of uncertainty resolution and induction in that they not only resolve some uncertain cases; they also add new uncertainty to others. Procedures are also in place for continuous uncertainty monitoring at every level, particularly starting with the nurses as an early warning system for the aberrant and what's different from the expected, proceeding upward through the ranks to higher administration levels as well.

Perhaps even more unusual is deliberate uncertainty induction by those at higher levels or from different disciplines—and even from outside experts—who come to the unit and raise probing and challenging questions about other possibilities than those already reported as under consideration.

"Noticing Something Different" about COVID-19

In a second example, an Emergency Medicine physician, Cameron Kyle-Sidell (K-S), was setting up and leading an additional ICU at a major acute care hospital in the Bronx for treatment of severe COVID-19 pneumonia—a raging, novel, almost-unknown and terrifying disease. In April 2020, COVID-19 infection rates attended by high mortality were skyrocketing and causing major hospital crises in hospitals all over New York City. Even with advanced intensive-care treatment, patient death rates were astonishing, hospital morgues overflowing.

Weick and Sutcliff's (2015) prescriptions for uncertainty in complexity apply in this example, too: Many unknown unknowns are not able to be quickly detected; keep asking yourself what's different! The presentation of severe COVID-19 effects on the lungs had many of the features of Acute Respiratory Distress Syndrome (ARDS), a potentially fatal condition characterized by severe hypoxia (low blood levels of oxygen) and extremely difficult rapid breathing. An internationally accepted description for ARDS was established, along with a standard protocol for treating it with an external mechanical ventilator that delivered specific volumes of air mixed with oxygen to the lungs at controlled high pressures during both patient inhalation and exhalation.

The clinical appearance of the often-fatal severe lung dysfunction observed in many COVID-19 patients was very similar to that found in typical ARDS. So an adaptation of the standard ARDS lung ventilation protocol was routinely used on COVID-19 patients whose blood oxygen levels fell far enough to be considered dangerous and require patient ventilation.

That protocol is what presented a serious problem for K-S. As an ER doctor, he saw many more different types of patients with ARDS at different stages of the disease in the hospital ER than those who worked constantly in the ICU. When Kyle-Sidell observed COVID-19 patients at different stages, he saw that something physiologically just didn't make sense. He continues (in close paraphrase):

When I initially started treating patients in ICU, I thought I was going to be treating acute respiratory distress syndrome (ARDS), similar to what I saw in AIDS, when I was a fellow. But, I hadn't seen patients with ARDS and very low blood oxygen levels who could talk in full sentences and not manifest overt shortness of breath. When we put in a breathing tube, they usually drop their oxygen levels very quickly and get some kind of reflexive response from the heart ... like tachycardia [a very high heart rate]—that we also weren't seeing. So, what I was seeing did not make sense!

That originally came to me when we had a patient who had hit our low-blood-oxygen "trigger" in the ARDS protocol to put in a breathing tube. Most of the time, when patients hit that level of hypoxia, they're in distress and can barely talk. But she *could*—and she did *not* want a breathing tube. So, she asked that we put it in at the last minute possible.

That was perplexing: When *was* the last minute possible? All my instincts as a physician—like looking to see if she tires out—none of the usual things occurred .... So I came to realize this condition is nothing I've ever seen before. And, I started to read to try to figure this odd clinical syndrome out.

Having noticed something importantly different than other physicians in the US, Dr. Kyle-Sidell had figured out—by himself—something that had only just been recognized in Europe—and not here reported—after their much longer experience with COVID-19 pneumonia. Specifically, that it had two different presentations: An earlier phase where the lungs are flexible and easily inflatable during breathing (like the walls of a soft balloon), and a later one where the lung walls have become somewhat rigid, making breathing very difficult and tiring. Both conditions cause hypoxia—but for different reasons. And patients in the early phase can breathe easily and survive much lower levels of blood oxygen for much longer than they can in the later one.

K-S decided it was wrong to treat patients in the earlier phase with the same standard ARDS protocol that was used on all patients because the high ventilation pressures that it required for rigid lungs in ARDS could actually damage the flexible lung walls of patients in the earlier phase. He strongly believed it would be appropriate to try a different ventilation procedure keeping oxygen levels very high but with much lower pressures to protect fragile flexible lungs.

Feeling he couldn't morally in a doctor–patient relationship continue the standard protocol that was used in all the hospital ICUs, he decided he had to step down from the ICU and began testing his own procedure on COVID-19 patients in the ER.

Writing from an ecological perspective, Nora Bateson (2022) notes that we need to move from planned change in the face of complexity to a focus on creating the conditions that leave the system ready for whatever change may come. She writes:

> When an organism responds to an event in its environment, it responds from the combining cauldron of experiences that have formed and in-formed it. Yet, to continue "*to be*" requires constant shifting and learning to *be* in new ways. In our exploration of "systemic change," it would seem that there is a process prior to the "change" that allows organisms to become *ready* to respond in new ways. This process of ready-ing may be what makes the subsequent "change" possible. Before the change, there is a prelude, a priming, a saturation of mutual learning between organisms through which pathways of possibility are produced; we can imagine this as a process of becoming ready to perceive and thereby respond in new ways. (p. 990)

In the ICU, we see structures that were put in place to both reduce and induce uncertainty, to build ad hoc networks of expertise, to notice differences in order that alternative paths could be revealed. These structures create a culture of readiness for change. Bateson adds, "This process is open-ended, always sensitizing, ever-learning and taking place within an already existing aggregate of perceptions" (Bateson, 2022, p. 990).

Bateson calls for thinking across contexts as another way to hold multiple possibilities in mind. In L&D, for example, thinking about a change across units, levels, geographies, etc., allows a more nuanced understanding of a potential direction. Bateson refers to a "side-by-side-ing"—holding multiple possibilities side by side to see what might emerge. Bateson says,

> This is a process that happens through having inputs side-by-side that reknit, coalesce and combine. Here the tautologies are tickled, and the habituated collusions are mutually learning to be in new shapes .... The "new" comes from the gapping—the side-by-side-ing—the way in which an arrangement of images or experiences, senses or inputs are producing relevance between them. Like a conversation in which the meaning is not said, but is made through the spaces between the inputs. (p. 998)

Ann Pendleton-Jullian (2020) refers to this as creating cognitive equity—again keeping multiple pathways open, resisting closure, or, as Weick and Sutcliffe (2015) say, resisting categorization as long as possible.

In our work, we identified constructs that create a learning culture—a culture with the characteristics that create a readiness for change and transformation. Fundamental to our understanding of change in organizations is that change is a learning process. What these examples illustrate is that this learning is not learning as we used to understand it. It is not based on fixed objectives, but open-ended, adaptive to the situation, the prior knowledge and potential needs of the learners, and more often than not, "mutual learning . . . through which pathways of possibility are produced" (Bateson, 2022, p. 990).

CONCLUSION

The term "VUCA" still captures the essence of this shifting terrain, although consultants and scholars have offered variations as time has passed. VUCA stands for: Volatile (fluctuation), Uncertain (unpredictability), Complex (interdependence), and Ambiguous (lacking clarity). The Center for Creative Leadership works with the idea of RUPT: Rapid, Unpredictable, Paradoxical, and Tangled. No matter what the acronym, the response calls for diagnosis and action to support flexibility and capability to make decisions in situations for which there is no certainty or clear response.

The isolation and creativity unleashed in the pandemic made more visible how much we rely on informal and incidental learning in our everyday work, particularly as a response to increasing complexity. So what does this mean as L&D professionals attempt to harness the adaptations created during the pandemic? At least one implication is that this learning is extremely valuable—especially if it is surfaced, scaffolded, vetted, and translated into practice. In a number of our studies of informal and incidental learning, respondents say they don't think of what is learned incidentally as really learning—unless it is in a book or a classroom. By more openly embracing this learning, we can begin to unleash the imagination. New knowledge, new approaches we've never dreamed of, new worlds of L&D, will have their source in the informal and incidental learning we harness today.

Our system learning survey—Dimensions of the Learning Organization Questionnaire—has helped countless organizations and institutions assess their learning culture to date, but what should we be measuring to assess learning culture in today's complex environment? To assess continuous learning, we might ask what is counted as learning (e.g., classroom hours vs. learning in the workflow)? How is interdependent learning recognized and rewarded? How much tolerance is there for ambiguity? Does the culture punish or expect taking calculated risks? Is imagination and what-if thinking prevalent? To assess inquiry and dialogue, we might examine the extent to which organizations value curiosity and prioritize informal interaction and inclusive conversations. Does inquiry pair rational argument with embodied knowing and intuition? For teaming and collaboration, does the culture provide for psychological safety, the bellwether of team performance? To what extent is collaboration supported by at-the-ready practices? To what extent do groups work across knowledge, ethnic/racial/geocultural boundaries? How skilled are leaders and employees at perspective taking and negotiating differences? What kinds of "knowing" are captured and shared? Is knowledge updated continually to respond to changes in context? We know that leaders who mentor and coach are key to performance. Are employees encouraged to pursue their personal purpose to contribute to the collective vision? Do leaders empower those they lead? Is shared leadership practiced? Do leaders learn from those at the edges of their networks as well as from inner circles? How frequently are the perspectives of internal and cross-boundary clients tapped for environmental scanning?

It is not possible to conclude this book with simple prescriptions for success in rethinking L&D in light of complexity. We have offered a complexity-infused journey through alternative perspectives on how L&D leaders in different kinds of businesses, government organizations, not-for-profits, institutions, and healthcare systems are experimenting with alternative ways of building learning capacity in individuals and systems. We thank the L&D leaders who offered these perspectives and examples.

The vignettes in this volume offer a glimpse of how practitioners have rethought learning and development in the face of unprecedented digital and workforce transformations. While we cannot say these stories presage the future, they are a testament to one of the most enduring aspects of the workplace learning and development profession—the sheer creativity and passion for meeting the needs of the learners and of the organizations they serve. We admire their work and are delighted to share it in these pages.

References

Agile Alliance (2022). *Agile Essentials.* Retrieved March 18, 2023, from https://www.agilealliance.org/agile101

Almagro, C., Anastasijevic Vuletic, A., Bersin, J., Boskma, W., Bucka-Lassen, K., Edmondson, A., Friedman, S., Gower, B., Hellström, R., Jones, R., Joshi, S., Lont, R., Murtomaa, M., Nikitas, C., Paynter, S., Pibernat, H., Polczyk, A., Hölttä, J., Rock, D., … Wylon, D. (2017). *Manifesto for HR Development.* Retrieved September 5, 2022, from https://www.agilehrmanifesto.org/

Arellano, C., Di Leonardo, A. & Felix, I. (2017). Using people analytics to drive business performance: A case study. *McKinsey Quarterly, 3,* 114–119.

Argyris, C. (1970). *Intervention theory and method: A behavioral science view.* Addison-Wesley.

Argyris, C. (1976). *Increasing leadership effectiveness.* John Wiley & Sons.

Argyris, C. (1982). *Reasoning, learning, and action.* Jossey-Bass.

Arrow, H., McGrath, H. E. & Berdahl, J. L. (2000). *Small groups as complex systems: Formation, coordination, development, and adaptation.* Sage Publications.

Ashby, W. R. (1991). Requisite variety and its implications for the control of complex systems. In G. J. Klir (ed.), *Facets of systems science* (pp. 405–417). Springer.

Autor, D. (2014). *Polanyi's paradox and the shape of employment growth.* Retrieved from https://www.nber.org/papers/w20485, n.d.

Avolio, B. J., Walumbwa, F. O. & Weber, T. J. (2009). Leadership: Current theories, research, and future directions. *Annual Review of Psychology, 60,* 421–449.

Baran, B. (1987). The technological transformation of white-collar work: A case study of the insurance industry. In H. Hartman (ed.), *Computer chips and paper clips: Technology and women's employment, 2,* 25–62.

Barley, S. R. (1996). Technicians in the workplace: Ethnographic evidence for bringing work into organizational studies. *Administrative Science Quarterly, 41*(3), 404–441.

Bass, B. M. & Avolio, B. J. (1989). *Manual for the multifactor leadership questionnaire.* Free Press; Consulting Psychologists Press.

Bateson, N. (2022). An essay on ready-ing: Tending the prelude to change. *Systems Research and Behavioral Science, 39*(4), 990–1004.

Beck, N. (1992). *Shifting gears: Thriving in the new economy.* HarperCollins.

Beck, U. (2000). *Brave new world of work.* Blackwell Publishers.

Beckhard, R. (2006). What is organization development? In J. V. Gallos (ed.), *Organization development: A Jossey-Bass reader* (pp. 3–12). Jossey-Bass; Wiley.

Bennis, W., Benne, K. & Chin, R. (1969) *The planning of change* (2nd edn). Rinehart & Winston, Inc.

Bersin, J. (2017). High impact learning organizations: Moving beyond L&D. *Executive Perspective.* Deloitte [online newspaper].

Bersin, J. (2018). A new paradigm for corporate training: Learning in the flow of work. *Josh Bersin: Insights on Corporate Talent, Learning, and HR Technology.* Retrieved March 18, 2023, from https://joshbersin.com/2018/06/a-new-paradigm-for-corporate-training-learning-in-the-flow-of-work/

Bhattarai, A. P. (2021). *A Foucauldian reading of the train the trainer literature* [unpublished doctoral dissertation]. The University of Georgia.

Bieke, S. & Maarten, D. L. (2012). Network awareness tool-learning analytics in the workplace: Detecting and analyzing informal workplace learning. In *Proceedings of the 2nd International Conference on Learning Analytics and Knowledge*, April (pp. 59–64). Association for Computing Machinery.

Bransford, J., Derry, S., Berliner, D., Hammerness, K. & Beckett, K. L. (2005). Theories of learning and their roles in teaching. In L. Darling-Hammond & J. Bransford (eds), *Preparing teachers for a changing world: What teachers should learn and be able to do* (pp. 40–87). John Wiley & Sons.

Brinkerhoff, R. (2003). *The success case method: Find out quickly what's working and what's not*. Berrett-Koehler Publishers.

Brinkerhoff, R. (2005). The success case method: A strategic evaluation approach to increasing the value and effect of training. *Advances in Developing Human Resources*, *7*(1), 86–101.

Broussard, M. (2018). *Artificial unintelligence: How computers misunderstand the world*. MIT Press.

Brown, J. S. & Thomas, D. (2009). Learning in/for a world of constant flux: Homo sapiens, Homo faber & Homo ludens revisited. In L. E. Weber & J. J. Duderstadt (eds), *University Research for Innovation, VII Glion Colloquium* (pp. 321–336). Economica.

Burke, W. & Litwin, G. (1992). A causal model of organizational performance and change. *Journal of Management*, *18*(3), 523–545.

Bushe, G. R. & Marshak, R. J. (2016). The dialogic organization development approach to transformation and change. In W. Rothwell, J. Stravros & R. Sullivan (eds), *Practicing organization development*, 4th edn (pp. 407–418). John Wiley & Sons.

Buterin, V. (2014). *DAOs, DACs, DAs and more: An incomplete terminology guide*. Ethereum.org, May 6. Retrieved September 24, 2022, from https://blog.ethereum.org/2014/05/06/daos-dacs-das-and-more-an-incomplete-terminology-guide

Buterin, V. (2021a). *Retroactive Public Goods Funding*. Medium, July 20. Retrieved September 24, 2022, from https://medium.com/ethereum-optimism/retroactive-public-goods-funding-33c9b7d00f0c

Buterin, V. (2021b). *Review of Optimism Retro Funding Round 1*, November 16. Retrieved September 24, 2022, from https://vitalik.ca/general/2021/11/16/retro1.html

Care, O., Bernstein, M. J., Chapman, M., Diaz Reviriego, I., Dressler, G., Felipe-Lucia, M. R., … & Zähringer, J. G. (2021). Creating leadership collectives for sustainability transformations. *Sustainability Science*, *16*(2), 703–708.

Carter, S. S. (2016). *The relationship between transformational leadership and organizational learning culture in magnet and non-magnet hospitals*. Northeastern University.

Center for Creative Leadership. (2020). *Direction + Alignment + Commitment (DAC) = Leadership*, November 22. Retrieved September 24, 2022, from https://www.ccl.org/articles/leading-effectively-articles/make-leadership-happen-with-dac-framework/

Cheng, Y. T. & Van de Ven, A. H. (1996). Learning the innovation journey: Order out of chaos? *Organization Science*, *7*(6), 593–614.

Clutterbuck, D. (2007). *Coaching the team at work: The definitive guide to team coaching*. Nicholas Brealey.

Coleman, P. T., Coon, D., Kim, R., Chung, C., Bass, R., Regan, B. & Anderson, R. (2017). Promoting constructive multicultural attractors: Fostering unity and fairness from diversity and conflict. *The Journal of Applied Behavioral Science*, *53*(2), 180–211.

Colombetti, G. & Thompson, E. (2007). The feeling body: Toward an enactive approach to emotion. In W. F. Overton, U Müller & J. L. Newman (eds), *Developmental perspectives on embodiment and consciousness* (pp. 61–84). Psychology Press.

Corrie, I., Lawson, R. & Rowland, T. (2020). Transformative action coaching in healthcare leadership. *Journal of Transformative Learning*, *6*(2), 39–51.

Crawford, K. (2021). *The atlas of AI*. Yale University Press.

Croft, C., McGivern, G., Currie, G., Lockett, A. & Spyridonidis, D. (2022). Unified divergence and the development of collective leadership. *Journal of Management Studies*, *59*(2), 460–488.

Cseh, M., Watkins, K. E. & Marsick, V. J. (1999). Re-conceptualizing Marsick and Watkins' model of informal and incidental learning in the workplace. In K. P. Kuchinke (ed.), *Proceedings of the Academy of HRD* (pp. 349–355). Academy of Human Resource Development.

Csikszentmihalyi, M. (1990). *Flow: The psychology of optimal experience*. Harper & Row.

Danaher, J. (2019). *Automation and Utopia: Human flourishing in a world without work*. Harvard University Press.

Dastin, J. (2018). *Amazon scraps secret AI recruiting tool that showed bias against women*. Reuters, October 9. Retrieved October 3, 2022, from https://www.reuters.com/article/us-amazon-com-jobs-automation-insight/amazon-scraps-secretai-recruiting-tool-that-showed-bias-against-womenidUSKCN1MK08G

Day, D. V., Fleenor, J. W., Atwater, L. E., Sturm, R. E. & McKee, R. A. (2014). Advances in leader and leadership development: A review of 25 years of research and theory. *The Leadership Quarterly*, *25*(1), 63–82.

De Laat, M. & Schreurs, B. (2013). Visualizing informal professional development networks: Building a case for learning analytics in the workplace. *American Behavioral Scientist*, *57*(10), 1421–1431.

de Romrée, H., Fecheyr-Lippens, B. & Schaninger, B. (2016). People analytics reveals three things HR may be getting wrong. *McKinsey Quarterly*. Retrieved October 3, 2022, from https://www.mckinsey.com/capabilities/people-and-organizational-performance/our-insights/people-analytics-reveals-three-things-hr-may-be-getting-wrong

Dechant, K., Marsick, V. J. & Kasl, E. (1993). Towards a model of team learning. *Studies in Continuing Education*, *15*(1), 1–14.

Decuyper, S., Dochy, F. & Van den Bossche, P. (2010). Grasping the dynamic complexity of team learning: An integrative model for effective team learning in organisations. *Educational Research Review*, *5*(2), 111–133.

DeLuca, J. R. (1999). *Political savvy: Systematic approaches to leadership behind-the-scenes*. Evergreen Business Group.

Denyer, D. & James, K. T. (2016). Doing leadership-as-practice development. In A. Raelin (ed.), *Leadership-as-practice* (pp. 262–283). Routledge.

Dewey, J. (1938). *Experience and education*. Collier Books.

Dixon, N. M. (1990). The relationship between trainee responses on participant reaction forms and posttest scores. *Human Resource Development Quarterly*, *1*(2), 129–137.

Edmondson, A. C. (1999). Psychological safety and learning behaviour in work teams. *Administrative Science Quarterly*, *44*(2), 350–383.

Edmondson, A. C. (2012). *Teaming: How organizations learn, innovate, and compete in the knowledge economy*. Jossey-Bass.

Edmondson, A. C. (2013). *Teaming to innovate*. Jossey-Bass.

Edmondson, A. C. & Harvey, J. F. (2017). *Extreme teaming: Lessons in complex, cross-sector leadership*. Emerald Publishing.

Edmondson, A. C. & Harvey, J. F. (2018). Cross-boundary teaming for innovation: Integrating research on teams and knowledge in organizations. *Human Resource Management Review*, *28*(4), 347–360.

Ellinger, A. D. & Bostrom, R. P. (2002). An examination of managers' beliefs about their roles as facilitators of learning. *Management Learning*, *33*(2), 147–179.

Ellinger, A. D. & Cseh, M. (2007). Contextual factors influencing the facilitation of others' learning through everyday work experiences. *Journal of Workplace Learning*, *19*(7), 435–452.

Ellinger, A. D., Ellinger, A. E., Yang, B. & Howton, S. W. (2002). The relationship between the learning organization concept and firms' financial performance: An empirical assessment. *Human Resource Development Quarterly*, *13*(1), 5–22.

Eraut, M. (2004). Informal learning in the workplace. *Studies in Continuing Education*, *26*(2), 247–273.

Ethereum-Optimism. (n.d.). *Ethereum-Optimism/Operating-Manual: Operating Manual of the Optimism Collective*. GitHub. Retrieved March 13, 2023, from https://github.com/ethereum-optimism/OPerating-manual

Ethereum.org. (2022). *Decentralized Autonomous Organizations (DAOs)*. Ethereum.org, October 14. Retrieved November 28, 2022, from https://ethereum.org/en/dao/

Eva, N., Cox, J. W., Herman, H. M. & Lowe, K. B. (2021). From competency to conversation: A multi-perspective approach to collective leadership development. *The Leadership Quarterly*, *32*(5), 101346.

Fairclough, N. (2003). *Analysing discourse: Textual analysis for social research*. Routledge.

Faller, P., Marsick, V. & Russell, C. (2020). Adapting action learning strategies to operationalize reflection in the workplace. *Advances in Developing Human Resources*, *22*(3), 291–307.

Fenwick, T. J. (2000). Expanding conceptions of experiential learning: A review of the five contemporary perspectives on cognition. *Adult Education Quarterly*, *50*(4), 243–272. https://doi.org/10.1177/07417130022087035

Flanagan, J. C. (1954). The critical incident technique. *Psychological Bulletin*, *51*, 327–358.

Freire, P. (1970). *Pedagogy of the oppressed*. Continuum International Publishing Group, Inc.

Frey, C. B. & Osborne, M. (2013). *The future of employment: How susceptible are jobs to computerization?* [working paper]. Published by the Oxford Martin Programme on Technology and Employment.

Frey, C. B. & Osborne, M. (2015). *Technology at work: The future of innovation and employment*. Citi GPS.

Friedrich, T. L., Vessey, W. B., Schuelke, M. J., Ruark, G. A. & Mumford, M. D. (2009). A framework for understanding collective leadership: The selective utilization of leader and team expertise within networks. *The Leadership Quarterly*, *20*(6), 933–958.

Gal, U., Jensen, T. B. & Stein, M. K. (2020). Breaking the vicious cycle of algorithmic management: A virtue ethics approach to people analytics. *Information and Organization*, *30*(2), 100301.

Gentile, M. C. (2014). Giving voice to values: An action-oriented approach to values-driven leadership. *SAM Advanced Management Journal*, *79*(4), 42–50.

Gephart, M. A. & Marsick, V. J. (2016). *Strategic organizational learning*. Springer.

Gergen, K. J. & Hersted, L. (2016). Developing leadership as dialogic practice. In J. A. Raelin (ed.), *Leadership-as-practice: Theory and application* (pp. 178–197). Routledge.

Gery, G. (1991). *Electronic Performance Support Systems*. Gery Associates.

Gherardi, S. (2000). Practice-based theorizing on learning and knowing in organizations. *Organization*, *7*(2), 211–223.

Giermindl, L. M., Strich, F., Christ, O., Leicht-Deobald, U. & Redzepi, A. (2022). The dark sides of people analytics: Reviewing the perils for organisations and employees. *European Journal of Information Systems*, *31*(3), 410–435. https://doi.org/10.1080/0960085X.2021.1927213

Glasner, E. & Weiss, B. (1993). Sensitive dependence on initial conditions. *Nonlinearity*, *6*(6), 1067–1075.

Glenn, E. N. & Feldberg, R. L. (1977). Degraded and deskilled: The proletarianization of clerical work. *Social Problems*, *25*(1), 52–64. https://doi.org/10.2307/800467

Goldman, E., Plack, M., Roche, C., Smith, J. & Turley, C. (2009). Learning in a chaotic environment. *Journal of Workplace Learning*, *21*(7), 555–574. https://doi.org/10.1108/13665620910985540

Gram-Hanssen, I. (2021). Individual and collective leadership for deliberate transformations: Insights from Indigenous leadership. *Leadership*, *17*(5), 519-541. https://doi.org/10.1177/1742715021996486

Hackman, J. R. (1990). *Groups that work*. Jossey-Bass.

Hagel III, J., Brown, J. S. & Davison, L. (2010). *The power of pull: How small moves, smartly made, can set big things in motion*. Basic Books.

Haigh, T. (2006). Remembering the office of the future: The origins of word processing and office automation. *IEEE Annals of the History of Computing*, *28*(4), 6–31. https://doi.org/10.1109/MAHC.2006.70

Harner, M. D. (2013). *Incidental learning in a complex clinical workplace* [doctoral dissertation]. Northern Illinois University.

Hawkins, P. & Turner, E. (2019). *Systemic coaching: Delivering value beyond the individual*. Routledge.

Heifetz, R., Grashow, A. & Linsky, M. (2009). *The practice of adaptive leadership*. Harvard Business School Publishing.

Hiipakka, J. (2018). *Prediction: Learning will go to where work happens*. Retrieved July 7, 2022, from https://capitalhblog.deloitte.com/2018/12/03/prediction-learning-will-go-to-where-work-happens/

Hofmann, E. & Rüsch, M. (2017). Industry 4.0 and the current status as well as future prospects on logistics. *Computers in Industry*, *89*, 23–34.

Holland, J. H. (1998). *Emergence: From chaos to complexity*. Perseus Books.

Homan, T. (2001). *Teamleren: Theorie en facilitatie*. Academic Service.

Hoque, Z. (2014). 20 years of studies on the balanced scorecard: Trends, accomplishments, gaps and opportunities for future research. *The British Accounting Review*, *46*(1), 33–59.

IBM (2006). Learning infrastructure: Architecting a formal and informal learning environment. Executive Brief, IBM Learning Solutions, G510-6471-00.

Jacobs, R. L. & Park, Y. (2009). A proposed conceptual framework of workplace learning: Implications for theory development and research in human resource development. *Human Resource Development Review*, *8*(2), 133–150.

Jimenez, R. (2019). *Workflow learning*. Monogatari Press; Vignetteslearning.com.
Jinks, J. (2022). *Incidental learning in complexity: measuring the roughness of learning.* [unpublished dissertation]. The University of Georgia.
Jinks, J. & Watkins, K. E. (2020). *The "secret sauce" in high performing stores in a fast food organization* [poster presentation]. Academy of Human Resource Development International Conference of the Americas, Atlanta, Georgia, USA.
Joksimovic, S., Siemens, G., Wang, Y. E., San Pedro, M. O. Z. & Way, J. (2020). Beyond cognitive ability. *Journal of Learning Analytics*, *7*(1), 1–4.
Ju, B., Lee, Y., Park, S. & Yoon, S. W. (2021). A meta-analytic review of the relationship between learning organization and organizational performance and employee attitudes: Using the Dimensions of the Learning Organization Questionnaire. *Human Resource Development Review*, *20*(2), 207–251.
Juarrero, A. (1999). *Dynamics in action.* MIT Press.
Jung, H., Kim, Y., Lee, H. & Shin, Y. (2019). Advanced instructional design for successive e-learning: Based on the successive approximation model (SAM). *International Journal on E-learning*, *18*(2), 191–204.
Justice, S., Morrison, E. & Yorks, L. (2020). Enacting reflection: A new approach to workplace complexities. *Advances in Developing Human Resources*, *22*(3), 320–332.
Kaplan, R. S. & Norton, D. P. (1992). The balanced scorecard: Measures that drive performance. *Harvard Business Review*, *70*(1), 71–79.
Kasl, E., Marsick, V. J. & Dechant, K. (1997). Teams as learners: A research-based model of team learning. *Journal of Applied Behavioral Science*, *33*(2), 227–246.
Kim, K. & Watkins, K. E. (2018). *Leaders' behaviors and organizational performance* [presentation]. University Forum for HRD, Northumbria, Newcastle, UK.
Kirkpatrick, D. L. (1983). Four steps to measuring training effectiveness. *Personnel Administrator*, *28*, 19–25.
Kirkpatrick, D. L. (1998). *Evaluating training programs: The four levels.* Berrett-Koehler.
Kolb, D. A. (1984). *Experiential learning: Experience as the source of learning and development*. Prentice-Hall.
Kuchinke, K. P. (1998). Moving beyond the dualism of performance versus learning: A response to Barrie and Pace. *Human Resource Development Quarterly*, *9*(4), 377–384.
Ladyman, J. & Wiesner, K. (2020). *What is a complex system?* Yale University Press.
Lang, S. (2013). *Leadership style and learning organization in banking industry: A study in head office of Canadia Bank Plc in Phnom Penh, Cambodia* [doctoral dissertation]. Burapha University, Thailand.
Lawrence, P. (2019). What is systemic coaching? *Philosophy of Coaching: An International Journal*, *4*(2), 35–52.
Leonardi, P. & Contractor, N. (2018). Better people analytics. *Harvard Business Review*, *96*(6), 70–81.
Lewin, K. (1946). Action research and minority problems. *Journal of Social Issues*, *2*(4), 34–46.
Lewin, K. (1947). Frontiers in group dynamics. *Human Relations*, *1*, 5–41.
Ley, T., Cook, J., Dennerlein, S., Kravcik, M., Kunzmann, C., Pata, K., … Trattner, C. (2014). Scaling informal learning at the workplace: A model and four designs from a large-scale design-based research effort. *British Journal of Educational Technology*, *45*(6), 1036–1048.

LinkedIn Learning (2019). *Third Annual 2019 Workplace Learning Report: Why 2019 is the breakout year for talent development*. LinkedIn Learning. Retrieved July 7, 2022, from https://learning.linkedin.com/content/dam/me/business/en-us/amp/learning-solutions/images/workplace-learning-report-2019/pdf/workplace-learning-report-2019.pdf

Lundberg, C. C. (1989). On organizational learning: Implications and opportunities for expanding organizational development. *Research in Organizational Change and Development*, *3*(6), 126–182.

Lundgren, H. & Poell, R. F. (2020). Human resource development and workplace learning. In T. S. Rocco, M. C. Smith, R. C. Mizzi, L. R. Merriweather & J. D. Hawley (eds), *The handbook of adult and continuing education* (pp. 275–286). AAACE.

Mallon, D. (Host). (2019). Learning in the flow of work [transcript of audio podcast]. Deloitte, January. Retrieved July 7, 2022, from https://www2.deloitte.com/us/en/pages/human-capital/articles/learning-in-the-flow-of-work-podcast.html

Marsick, V.J. (1987). *Learning in the workplace*. Croom Helm.

Marsick, V. J. & O'Neil, J. (2009). Peer mentoring and action learning. *Adult Learning*, *20*(1 & 2), 19–24.

Marsick, V. J. & Watkins, K. E. (1990/2015). *Informal and incidental learning in the workplace*. Routledge & Kegan Paul.

Marsick, V. J. & Watkins, K. E. (1996). Adult educators and the challenge of the learning organization. *Adult Learning*, *7*(4), 18–20.

Marsick, V. J. & Watkins, K. E. (1999). *Facilitating learning organizations: Making learning count*. Gower Publishing, Ltd.

Marsick, V. J. & Watkins, K. E. (2003). Demonstrating the value of an organization's learning culture: The dimensions of the learning organization questionnaire. *Advances in Developing Human Resources*, *5*(2), 132–151.

Marsick, V. J., Fichter, R. & Watkins, K. E. (2021). From work-based learning to learning-based work: Exploring the changing relationship between learning and work. In M. Malloch, L. Cairns, B. O'Connor & K. Evans (eds), *The Sage handbook of learning and work* (pp. 177–193). Sage Publications.

Marsick, V. J., Watkins, K. E., Scully-Russ, E. & Nicolaides, A. (2017). Rethinking informal and incidental learning in terms of complexity and the social context. *Journal of Adult Learning, Knowledge and Innovation*, *1*(1), 27–34.

Mattox II, J. R., Van Buren, M. & Martin, J. (2016). *Learning analytics: Measurement innovations to support employee development*. Kogan Page Publishers.

McClellan, D. (1983). Towards a general model of collective learning: A critique of existing models of specific social systems and a sketch of a model for social systems in general [unpublished doctoral dissertation]. University of Massachusetts, Boston, USA.

Meyer, A. D. (1982). Adapting to environmental jolts. *Administrative Science Quarterly*, *27*(4), 515–537.

Mezirow, J. (1978). Perspective transformation. *Adult Education*, *28*(2), 100–110.

Mitchell, M. (2009). *Complexity: A guided tour*. Oxford University Press.

Murray, P. J. (1998). Complexity theory and the fifth discipline. *Systemic Practice and Action Research*, *11*(3), 275–293.

National Academies of Sciences, Engineering, and Medicine. (2018). *How people learn II: Learners, contexts, and cultures*. The National Academies Press. https://doi.org/10.17226/24763

Neaman, A. & Marsick, V. J. (2018). Integrating learning into work: Design the context, not just the technology. In D. Mentor (ed.), *Computer-mediated learning for workforce development* (pp. 1–21). IGI Global.
Nichols, T. & Beynon, H. (1977). *Living with capitalism: Class relations and the modern factory*. Routledge & Kegan Paul.
North America Primary Care Research Group (n.d.). Retrieved October 21, 2022, from www.napcrg.org
O'Neil, J. & Marsick, V. J. (2007). *Understanding action learning* (AMA Innovations in Adult Learning). AMACOM.
Optimism. (2022a). *Welcome to the Optimism Collective Discourse!* gov.optimism.io, February 11. Retrieved September 25, 2022, from https://gov.optimism.io/t/welcome-to-the-optimism-collective-discourse/7
Optimism. (2022b). *Working Constitution of the Optimism Collective*. Optimism.io. Retrieved September 25, 2022, from https://gov.optimism.io/t/working-constitution-of-the-optimism-collective/55
Organization for Economic Cooperation and Development (2019). OECD Skills Strategy 2019: Skills to shape a better future. Retrieved October 12, 2020, from https://www.oecd-ilibrary.org/education/oecd-skills-strategy-2019_9789264313835-en
Ospina, S. M., Foldy, E. G., Fairhurst, G. T. & Jackson, B. (2020). Collective dimensions of leadership: connecting theory and method. *Human Relations*, *73*(4), 441–463.
Oxford English Dictionary. (1989). Oxford University Press.
Papanagnou, D., Watkins, K. E., Lundgren, H., Alcid, G. A., Ziring, D. & Marsick, V. J. (2022). Informal and incidental learning in the clinical learning environment: Learning through complexity and uncertainty during COVID-19. *Academic Medicine: Journal of the Association of American Medical Colleges*, *97*(8), 1137–1143.
Patton, M. Q. (2011). *Developmental evaluation: Applying complexity concepts to enhance innovation and use*. Guilford Press.
Pendleton-Jullian, A. M. (2020). An interview with Ann Pendleton-Jullian, University of Georgia Generative Learning and Complexity Laboratory. Retrieved March 19, 2023, from https://www.youtube.com/watch?v=JlaBxHTetbk
Pendleton-Jullian, A. M. & Brown, J. S. (2018a). *Design unbound: Designing for emergence in a white water world, Volume 1: Designing for emergence*. MIT Press.
Pendleton-Jullian, A. M. & Brown, J. S. (2018b). *Design unbound: Designing for emergence in a white water world, Volume 2: Ecologies of change*. MIT Press.
Phillips, J. J. (1998). Measuring the return on investment in organization development: Key issues and trends. *Organization Development Journal*, *16*(4). Retrieved March 19, 2023, from https://www.roiinstitute.net/wp-content/uploads/2018/03/Measuring-ROI-The-ProcessCurrent-Issues-and-Trends.pdf
Pimapunsri, P. (2014). Learning organization and leadership style in Thailand. *The Business & Management Review*, *4*(4), 7–12.
Poell, R., Chivers, G. E., Van der Krogt, F. J. & Wildemeersch, D. A. (2000). Learning-network theory: Organizing the dynamic relationships between learning and work. *Management Learning*, *31*(1) 25–49.
Poell, R. F., Lundgren, H., Bang, A., Justice, S., Marsick, V., Sung, S. Y. & Yorks, L. (2018). How do employees' individual learning paths differ across occupations? A review of 10 years of empirical research. *Journal of Workplace Learning*, *30*(5), 315–334.

Polanyi, M. (1966/2009). *The tacit dimension*. University of Chicago Press.
Raelin, J. A. (2016). Introduction to leadership-as-practice: Theory and application. In *Leadership-as-practice* (pp. 1–17). Routledge.
Reber, A. S. (1993). *Implicit learning and tacit knowledge: An essay on the cognitive unconscious*. Oxford University Press.
Reischmann, J. (1986). Learning "en passant": The forgotten dimension [paper presentation]. *American Association for Adult and Continuing Education*. Hollywood, FL, USA.
Robbins, S. E. (2020). Team learning as boundary crossing: incubating collaboration. *Human Resource Development International*. https://doi.org/10.1080/13678868.2020.1790254
Robinson, E. (2021). *Learning and performance during implementation of an innovative project: A single case study of a cross-functional team within a scientific communications agency* [dissertation]. Teachers College, Columbia University, New York, USA.
Rogers, E. M., Medina, U. E., Rivera, M. A. & Wiley, C. J. (2005). Complex adaptive systems and the diffusion of innovations. *The Innovation Journal: The Public Sector Innovation Journal*, *10*(3), 1–26.
Rosenblat, A. (2018). *Uberland: How algorithms are rewriting the rules of work*. University of California Press.
Ruiz-Calleja, A., Prieto, L. P., Ley, T., Rodríguez-Triana, M. J. & Dennerlein, S. (2017). Learning analytics for professional and workplace learning: A literature review. In *European Conference on Technology Enhanced Learning* (pp. 164–178). Springer International.
Santana, C. & Albareda, L. (2022). Blockchain and the emergence of Decentralized Autonomous Organizations (DAOs): An integrative model and research agenda. *Technological Forecasting and Social Change*, *182*, 121806.
Scharmer, C. O. (2009). *Theory U: Learning from the future as it emerges*. Berrett-Koehler Publishers.
Schön, D. A. (1984). *The reflective practitioner: How professionals think in action* (vol. 5126). Basic Books.
Schreyögg, G. & Ostermann, S. M. (2014). *Managing uncertainty in intensive care units: Exploring formal and informal coping practices in a university hospital*. Diskussionsbeiträge (no. 2014/14), Freie Universität Berlin, Fachbereich Wirtschaftswissenschaft, Berlin.
Schwab, K. (2017). *The fourth industrial revolution*. Currency.
Schwab, K. & Malleret, T. (2020). *COVID-19: The great reset*. ISBN Agentur Schweiz.
Scully-Russ, E. & Boyle, K. (2018). Sowing the seeds of change: Equitable food initiative through the lens of Vygotsky's cultural–historical development theory. *New Directions for Adult and Continuing Education*, *2018*(159), 37–52.
Senge, P. M. (1990). *The art and practice of the learning organization* (vol. 1). Doubleday.
Senge, P. M. (1997). The fifth discipline. *Measuring Business Excellence*, *1*(3), 46–51.
Siemens, G. (2004). Connectivism: A learning theory for the digital age. Retrieved June 4, 2022, from htttp://www.elearnspace.org
Siemens, G. (2022). *It's networks all the way down*. Presentation to The Geneva Learning Foundation Partnership workshop.
Silva, P. (2007). *Epistemology of incidental learning* [doctoral dissertation]. Virginia Tech, Blacksburg, Virginia, USA.

Simon, H. A. (1965). Administrative decision making. *Public Administration Review*, *25*(1), 31–37.

Sinek, S. (2019). *The infinite game*. Penguin.

Sleeva, S. L. (2021). *Agile innovation team learning: A multiple case study of agile software development teams* [published doctoral dissertation]. Teachers College, Columbia University ProQuest Dissertations Publishing. https://doi.org/10.7916/d8-mr98-jv77

Smith, V. (2001). *Crossing the great divide: Worker risk and opportunity in the new economy*. Cornell University Press.

Snowden, D. J. & Boone, M. E. (2007). A leader's framework for decision making. *Harvard Business Review*, *85*(11). Retrieved March 19, 2023, from https://hbr.org/2007/11/a-leaders-framework-for-decision-making

Stiegler, B. (2016). *Automatic society volume 1: The future of work* (trans. D. Ross). Polity.

Swanson, R. A. (2022). *Foundations of human resource development*. Berrett-Koehler Publishers.

Taber, N., Plumb, D. & Jolemore, S. (2008). "Grey" areas and "organized chaos" in emergency response. *Journal of Workplace Learning*, *20*(4), 272–285.

Tamkin, P., Yarnall, J. & Kerrin, M. (2002). *Kirkpatrick and beyond: A review of models of training evaluation*. Institute for Employment Studies.

Taylor, K. & Marienau, C. (2016). *Facilitating learning with the adult brain in mind*. Jossey-Bass.

The Evaluation Forum. (2003). Guide to evaluating leadership development programs. Retrieved November 10, 2010, from http://www.capacity.org/en/resource_corners/leadership/tools _methods/tools_methods_guide_to_evaluating_leadership_development_programs

The Geneva Learning Foundation. (2022). *Immunization Agenda 2030 Case Study*. Geneva.

Thietart, R.-A. & Forgues, B. (1997). Action, structure and chaos. *Organization Studies*, *18*(1), 119–143.

Tursunbayeva, A., Di Lauro, S. & Pagliari, C. (2018). People analytics—A scoping review of conceptual boundaries and value propositions. *International Journal of Information Management*, *43*, 224–247.

Vygotsky, L. S. (1978) *Mind in society: The development of higher mental processes*. Harvard University Press.

Warr, P., Allan, C. & Birdi, K. (1999). Predicting three levels of training outcome. *Journal of Occupational and Organizational Psychology*, *72*(3), 351–375.

Watkins, K. E. (1989). Business and industry. In P. Cunningham and S. Merriam (eds), *Handbook of adult and continuing education* (pp. 422–435). Jossey-Bass.

Watkins, K. E. & Dirani, K. M. (2013). A meta-analysis of the dimensions of a learning organization questionnaire: Looking across cultures, ranks, and industries. *Advances in Developing Human Resources*, *15*(2), 148–162.

Watkins, K. E. & Kim, K. (2018). Current status and promising directions for research on the learning organization. *Human Resource Development Quarterly*, *29*(1), 15–29.

Watkins, K. E. & Marsick, V. J. (1993). *Sculpting the learning organization: Lessons in the art and science of systemic change*. Jossey-Bass.

Watkins, K. E. & Marsick, V. J. (1996). *In action: Creating the learning organization*. American Society for Training and Development.

Watkins, K. E. & Marsick, V. J. (1997). *Dimensions of the learning organization questionnaire*. Partners for the Learning Organization.
Watkins, K. E. & Marsick, V. J. (2016). Development of academic programs in human resource development in the United States. *Advances in Developing Human Resources*, *18*(4), 467–480.
Watkins, K. E., Lysø, I. H. & deMarrais, K. (2011). Evaluating executive leadership programs: A theory of change approach. *Advances in Developing Human Resources*, *13*(2), 208–239.
Weick, K. E. & Sutcliffe, K. M. (2015). *Managing the unexpected*. John Wiley & Sons.
Wheatley, M. (2011). *Leadership and the new science: Discovering order in a chaotic world* (3rd edn). Berrett Koehler.
Wheatley, M. & Frieze, D. (2006). Using emergence to take social innovation to scale. *The Berkana Institute*, *9*(3), 147–197.
Xie, L. (2020). The impact of servant leadership and transformational leadership on learning organization: A comparative analysis. *Leadership & Organization Development Journal*, *41*(2), 220–236.
Yammarino, F. J., Salas, E., Serban, A., Shirreffs, K. & Shuffler, M. L. (2012). Collectivistic leadership approaches: Putting the "we" in leadership science and practice. *Industrial and Organizational Psychology*, *5*(4), 382–402.

Index